DECISIONS AT
KENNESAW MOUNTAIN

OTHER BOOKS IN THE COMMAND DECISIONS IN AMERICA'S CIVIL WAR SERIES

Decisions at Stones River
Matt Spruill and Lee Spruill

Decisions at Second Manassas
Matt Spruill III and Matt Spruill IV

Decisions at Chickamauga
Dave Powell

Decisions at Chattanooga
Larry Peterson

Decisions of the Atlanta Campaign
Larry Peterson

Decisions of the 1862 Kentucky Campaign
Larry Peterson

Decisions at The Wilderness and Spotsylvania Court House
Dave Townsend

Decisions at Gettysburg, Second Edition
Matt Spruill

Decisions of the Tullahoma Campaign
Michael R. Bradley

Decisions at Antietam
Michael S. Lang

Decisions of the Seven Days
Matt Spruill

Decisions at Fredericksburg
Chris Mackowski

Decisions at Perryville
Larry Peterson

Decisions of the Maryland Campaign
Michael S. Lang

Decisions at Shiloh
Dave Powell

Decisions at Franklin
Andrew S. Bledsoe

Decisions of the 1862 Shenandoah Valley Campaign
Robert Tanner

DECISIONS
AT
KENNESAW MOUNTAIN

The Eleven Critical Decisions
That Defined the Battle

Larry Peterson

Maps by Matt Spruill

COMMAND DECISIONS
IN AMERICA'S CIVIL WAR
Matt Spruill and Larry Peterson,
Series Editors

The University of Tennessee Press / Knoxville

Copyright © 2023 by The University of Tennessee Press / Knoxville.
All Rights Reserved. Manufactured in the United States of America.
First Edition.

Library of Congress Cataloging-in-Publication Data

Names: Peterson, Lawrence K., author. | Spruill, Matt, cartographer.
Title: Decisions at Kennesaw Mountain : the eleven critical decisions that defined the battle / Larry Peterson ; maps by Matt Spruill
Other titles: Eleven critical decisions that defined the battle | Command decisions in America's Civil War.
Description: First edition. | Knoxville : The University of Tennessee Press, [2023] | Series: Command decisions in America's Civil War |Includes bibliographical references and index. | Summary: "As General William Tecumseh Sherman set his sights on Atlanta in the summer of 1864, he fought several small battles— Resaca, Pickett's Mill, and skirmishes around Marietta—against an ever-retreating General Joseph E. Johnston who had replaced the beleaguered General Braxton Bragg as leader of the Confederate Army of Tennessee. After heavy rains slowed Sherman's advance, Johnston shored his army up along the Brushy Mountain line. With Johnston's army well entrenched and Sherman unable to flank him because of the mountains and impassable roads, Sherman noted in his reports to Washington, 'Kennesaw is the key to the whole country.' Intended for the Command Decisions in America's Civil War series, this book explores eleven critical decisions that affected the outcome of the Battle of Kennesaw Mountain and why the battle unfolded as it did"—Provided by publisher.
Identifiers: LCCN 2023012311 (print) | LCCN 2023012312 (ebook) | ISBN 9781621908111 (paperback) | ISBN 9781621908128 (kindle edition) | ISBN 9781621908135 (pdf)
Subjects: LCSH: Kennesaw Mountain, Battle of, Ga., 1864. | Georgia—History—Civil War, 1861–1865.
Classification: LCC E476.7 .P47 2023 (print) | LCC E476.7 (ebook) | DDC 973.7/371—dc23/eng/20230322
LC record available at https://lccn.loc.gov/2023012311
LC ebook record available at https://lccn.loc.gov/2023012312

*To the soldiers on both sides, including my Great-Great-Grandfather,
Confederate Brigadier General Alfred J. Vaughan Jr.,
who fought at The Battle of Kennesaw Mountain, June 27, 1864.*

CONTENTS

Preface	xi
Acknowledgments	xvii
Introduction	1
Chapter 1. Before the Battle of Kennesaw Mountain, June 14–26, 1864	15
Chapter 2. The Battle of Kolb's Farm, June 21–22, 1864	31
Chapter 3. The Battle of Kennesaw Mountain, June 27, 1864	41
Chapter 4. After the Battle of Kennesaw Mountain, June 28–July 3, 1864	59
Chapter 5. Aftermath and Conclusions	63
Appendix I. Driving Tour of the Critical Decisions of the Battle of Kennesaw Mountain	71
Appendix II. Union Order of Battle	111
Appendix III. Confederate Order of Battle	135
Notes	153
Bibliography	169
Index	175

ILLUSTRATIONS

Photographs

Gen. Joseph E. Johnston, CSA	16
Big and Little Kennesaw Mountains	20
Maj. Gen. William T. Sherman, USA	21
The Dead Angle, Cheatham Hill, Kennesaw Mountain National Battlefield Park (KMNBP)	22
Maj. Gen. Benjamin F. Cheatham, CSA	23
Military crest versus topographical crest	25
Confederates dragging guns up Kennesaw Mountain	29
Lieut. Gen. John B. Hood, CSA	35
Brig. Gen. Charles G. Harker, USA	46
Col. Daniel McCook Jr., USA	52
Brig. Gen. Alfred J. Vaughan Jr., CSA	53
Brig. Gen. George Maney, CSA	54
Illinois Monument and tunnel entrance, KMNBP	56
Visitor Center, KMNBP	73
Pine Mountain, Kennesaw, GA	78
Kolb's Farm, KMNBP	83
Sherman's Headquarters, KMNBP	88

Thomas's Headquarters, KMNBP	91
Vaughan's position, the Dead Angle, Cheatham Hill, KMNBP	95
Pigeon Hill, KMNBP	102
Marietta Confederate Cemetery	106
Marietta National Cemetery	107

Maps

The Western Theater, 1861–1863	4
The Atlanta Campaign, May 7–June 27, 1864	11
Confederate Mountain Lines, June 5–18, 1864	17
Kennesaw Mountain Lines, June 22, 1864	19
Battle of Kolb's Farm, June 22, 1864	39
Overview, Battle of Kennesaw Mountain, June 27, 1864	45
Union Assault on Pigeon Hill, June 27, 1864	49
Union Assault on Cheatham Hill (the Dead Angle), June 27, 1864	51
Sherman Outflanks Johnston, July 2, 1864	61
Driving Tour of the Critical Decisions of the Battle of Kennesaw Mountain	70
Driving Tour Stop 1: Kennesaw Mountain National Battlefield Park Visitor Center	72
Driving Tour Stop 2: The Western and Atlantic Railroad Depot	75
Driving Tour Stop 3: Pine Mountain and Polk Monument	79
Driving Tour Stop 4: The Battle of Kolb's Farm	82
Driving Tour Stops 5A and 5B: Sherman's Headquarters	87
Driving Tour Stop 6: Cheatham Hill / Dead Angle	93
Driving Tour Stop 7: Pigeon Hill	99
Driving Tour Stop 8: Marietta Confederate Cemetery	105
Driving Tour Stop 9: Marietta National Cemetery	108

PREFACE

Similar to many readers of this book, I grew up fascinated by the Civil War. I read books on it and particularly enjoyed several TV shows depicting it. Further motivation was that I grew up knowing that my great-great-grandfather, Alfred Jefferson Vaughan Jr., participated in the war, ultimately appointed to the rank of brigadier general. How many can say that they are a descendent of a Confederate general!

My introduction to Kennesaw Mountain National Battlefield Park occurred on June 25, 1986 (two days before the anniversary of the battle). As a corporate pilot at that time based at DEN (Denver International Airport-the old Stapleton Airport), I flew from BDL (Bradley International Airport, near Hartford, Connecticut) into Atlanta's now Hartsfield-Jackson Atlanta International Airport the day before on a Dassault Falcon Jet 200, registration number N28U (from my logbook). The next day the other pilot, Marv Craig, and I drove to the battlefield and briefly toured it. I remember being impressed with the entrenchments there, I believe at Pigeon Hill. Little did I know how much my great-great grandfather Vaughan was connected to this battlefield.

Around 1995 I decided to research and write a biography about my ancestor general. This culminated in my book *Confederate Combat Commander: The Remarkable Life of Brigadier General Alfred J. Vaughan Jr.*, published in 2013 by the University of Tennessee Press. During this research, only then did I discover that he had not only been positioned on the Kennesaw Mountain battlefield, but he and his brigade actually directly defended the "Dead Angle" on

Preface

June 27, 1864. Finally on April 20, 2004 I visited the battlefield and especially the Dead Angle on Cheatham Hill and walked where General Vaughan had himself walked as he prepared his defenses and fought the battle.

As described in my preface for *Decisions at Perryville*, University of Tennessee Press editor Thomas Wells, Command Decisions in America's Civil War series coeditor Matt Spruill, and I agreed that books addressing the critical decisions made during a military campaign can also focus on one or more battles within that operation. In the case of the Atlanta Campaign, nine or ten battles are generally agreed to have taken place. Obviously, we cannot delve into the critical decisions of these individual engagements while working within the context of the campaign. This book is another attempt to explore a well-known battle within the push for Atlanta.[1]

Although not necessary, knowledge of the Atlanta Campaign fought from May through early September 1864 is helpful to place the Battle of Kennesaw Mountain in perspective. The introduction of this book will bring the reader up to date on actions prior to this fighting and leading up to the point at which critical decisions began to be made.[2]

The Command Decisions in America's Civil War series focuses on why a battle or campaign evolved the way it did, as opposed to what happened. The works in this series provide readers with an easy-to-grasp overview of events. With this understanding, readers may then delve more into the minutiae found in many books describing a battle or campaign. For instance, while providing an interesting, poignant story, a soldier's premonition of death seldom modified the outcome of an engagement. Consider the books in this series more like guidebooks than detailed textbooks including details such as a serviceman's foreboding.

In order to reinforce this concept, I define a critical decision as one directly affecting a battle or campaign from that time forward. While there are many, many choices made every day within an active army, these are the result of a few critical decisions. See the following chart depicting the levels of decisions:

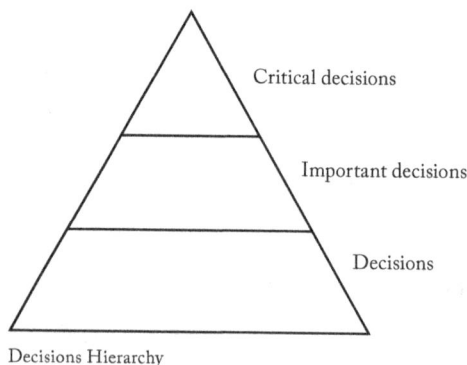

Decisions Hierarchy

xii

Typically only a handful of decisions qualify as critical. Some are obvious, but others are not.

The Battle of Kennesaw Mountain was one of the few times in the Atlanta Campaign when Maj. Gen. William T. Sherman decided to assault a well-established and well-fortified defensive line. He did order several attacks at the Battle of Resaca, but these were more like feints sizing up the Confederate Army of Tennessee while Sherman worked to successfully outflank and turn rebel commander Gen. Joseph E. Johnston out of that location. Sherman ordered direct assaults at New Hope Church, Pickett's Mill, and Utoy Creek, all generally involving fewer men than at Kennesaw Mountain. The Union officer also ordered a successful assault at Jonesboro the day before replacement commander Gen. John B. Hood abandoned Atlanta. In this situation six Union corps were available to attack the one Confederate corps present with minimum fortifications.

As most every soldier by then knew, Sherman learned at Kennesaw that there was virtually no chance of successfully assaulting and overrunning a well-entrenched enemy. Within two hours or so of a halt, both sides would establish strong enough fortifications to repel an offensive. By the next day the fortifications were too strong for any chance of a successful attack.

After Hood replaced Johnston, who had failed to halt Sherman's steady advance toward Atlanta, the new rebel commander ordered two assaults on various Union armies. Significantly, Hood attempted to catch enemy troops while they were not entrenched, but even then, the Yankees were able to erect rudimentary entrenchments at the Battles of Peachtree Creek and Atlanta. At the Battle of Ezra Church, Hood's subordinate Lieut. Gen Stephen D. Lee attacked a Union corps that had had only two hours to prepare for an onslaught. The Confederates lost some three thousand irreplaceable soldiers and were soundly repulsed.

This work presents and discusses critical decisions by first reviewing the situation pertaining to an upcoming choice. After discussing the options available to the decision-maker, I show the actual critical decision. Finally, I analyze the results and impact of the decision after it was made, indicating its effect on the rest of the battle.

The text is organized in four chronological chapters with the critical decisions pertaining to each listed below, plus a fifth chapter of analysis and a summary of events occurring as a result of the battle.

Chapter 1, "Before the Battle of Kennesaw Mountain, June 14–26, 1864," describes the five critical decisions that set the stage for the Battle of Kennesaw Mountain.

> Johnston Abandons the Mud Creek Line and Retreats to the Kennesaw Mountain Line
> Cheatham Decides to Defend a Salient in the Kennesaw Mountain Line
> Confederate Engineers Use the Topographical Crest Instead of the Military Crest
> Cheatham Carefully Locates and Camouflages His Artillery
> Confederate Artillery Is Dragged to the Top of Big and Little Kennesaw Mountains

Chapter 2, "The Battle of Kolb's Farm, June 21–22, 1864," covers the three critical decisions that resulted in this small engagement prior to Sherman's main attack five days later.

> Sherman Attempts to Outflank Johnston's Left Flank
> Johnston Orders Hood to Protect the Left Flank
> Hood Orders an Attack on the Newly Deployed Union Right Flank

Chapter 3, "The Battle of Kennesaw Mountain, June 27, 1864," discusses the two critical decisions that initially led to Union defeat, but also re-formed part of the Union line.

> Sherman Orders an Assault on the Center of the Kennesaw Mountain Line
> Union Commanders Assault Using Columns of Brigades

Chapter 4, "After the Battle of Kennesaw Mountain, June 28–July 3, 1864," examines Sherman's critical decision to resort back to outflanking Johnston.

> Sherman Outflanks Johnston to Advance toward the Chattahoochee River

To give readers a sense of what the various decision-makers actually faced, appendix I includes a driving tour of the locations of many of the critical decisions. This is not necessarily a tour of the battle, but it certainly traces parts of the engagement. Being on the same ground and in the same locations where decision-makers once were provides insight into what these individuals saw and faced. This practice can also be invaluable in understanding how a battle unfolded. Appendices II and III include the Union and Confederate orders of battle for the small Battle of Kolb's Farm, which preceded the main Battle of Kennesaw Mountain, and then the order of battle for that action. These allow readers to quickly access information about where particular units were placed within the various armies' structures.

Preface

Please be aware of several descriptions that appear in this book. The word Kennesaw was spelled with only one *n* at the time of the Civil War. For simplicity I use the modern spelling with two *n*s. As noted in the text, the well-known Pigeon Mountain was dubbed Kenesaw Spur during the war. In addition, this series uses abbreviations of military rank that the US Army employed during the Civil War, not the modern ones. Finally, Union corps were not represented by roman numerals until many years after the conflict. While books in this series spell out corps numbers as in *The War of the Rebellion: A Compilation of the Official Records of the Union and Confederate Armies*, roman numerals may appear on maps to conserve space and for ease of understanding.

ACKNOWLEDGMENTS

Many persons directly and indirectly assisted in the publication of *Decisions at Kennesaw Mountain*. First, I want to recognize many of the Atlanta Campaign historians who have provided the necessary background for this work. These include Albert Castel, Ed Bearss, Thomas Connelly, Larry Daniel, Stephen Davis, Earl Hess, Stanley Horn, Richard McMurry, William Scaife, and Steven Woodworth.

While researching my book on my great-great-grandfather Confederate brigadier general Alfred J. Vaughan Jr., I was fortunate to discover the Georgia Battlefields Association (GBA; georgiabattlefields.org), which focuses on the Civil War. Col. Charlie Crawford (USAF retired), the organization's longtime president, has spent countless hours driving me to the many relevant locations of the Atlanta Campaign, and helping me to make sense of it all. Bill Gurry, the association's current treasurer and a volunteer at Kennesaw Mountain National Battlefield Park, has helped by answering several specific questions and providing pictures. The annual GBA tour, which my wife, Kathleen, and I have usually attended for many years, and until just recently with Ed Bearss and Charlie as guides, has allowed me to obtain a much better grasp of the Atlanta Campaign.

The staff at the University of Tennessee Press continues to support me and this series. Thanks to director Scott Danforth, acquisitions editor Thomas Wells, editorial assistant Jon Boggs, marketing assistant Linsey Perry, production coordinator Stephanie Thompson, and publicist Tom Post for all of their patience and assistance. Special thanks to copyeditor Elizabeth Crowder for turning the manuscript into something readable.

My coeditor, mentor, and friend Col. Matt Spruill (US Army) deserves recognition for the help he has provided over the years on this and all of my other books. Thanks to his wife, Kathy, for loaning him out.

Speaking of wives, thanks once again to Kathleen for her continued support while I spend hour after hour at the computer, and for her company while I'm in the field.

Finally, I would like to thank my longtime friend and current president of the American Battlefield Trust (formerly the Civil War Trust) David Duncan for his dedication to preserving many Civil War battlefields. If you are not already, please consider becoming a member of the trust, and visit the organization's website at battlefields.org.

DECISIONS AT
KENNESAW MOUNTAIN

INTRODUCTION

By 1864 the Union and the Confederacy had fought the American Civil War for more than three years. Frustrated, many on the side of the Union began to believe that peace should be made with the Southern states in order to end the carnage. The rebels continued to hold out hope that the North would tire of the endless fighting and simply let the Confederacy secede. Any military advantage the Confederacy held had long since evaporated, as the industrial might of the Union showed itself more and more.[1]

In the Eastern Theater, the fighting largely took place between the two capitals at Washington, DC, and Richmond, Virginia, and, encouraged by Union president Abraham Lincoln and Confederate president Jefferson Davis, the First Battle of Bull Run, or Manassas, was fought on July 21, 1861. Though the engagement was initially a Union success, the Confederates turned it into a victory. However, both sides realized that they needed to conduct extensive training, procure appropriate weapons and ammunition, and standardize uniforms and flags. As a result, no significant fighting took place the rest of the year.[2]

Recognizing that his armies needed extensive organization, training, and equipage, Lincoln appointed Maj. Gen. George B. McClellan to overall command. After whipping the Army of the Potomac into a well-drilled organization, in the spring McClellan transported his force by ship to the mouth of the Rappahannock River. From there he cautiously advanced to the outskirts of Richmond. After Confederate commander Gen. Joseph E. Johnston was wounded during the Battle of Seven Pines, or Fair Oaks, Gen. Robert E. Lee assumed control of the rebel army. In a series of battles labeled the Seven Days, which began on June 25, 1862, Lee emerged victorious and forced McClellan back to Washington, DC. Lee advanced northeast and defeated Maj. Gen. John Pope's newly constituted Army of Virginia at the Second Battle of Manassas at the end of August. Lee then entered Maryland, carrying the war into Union territory. After a series of maneuvers, he and McClellan confronted each other near Sharpsburg, where the Battle of Antietam, or Sharpsburg, took place on September 17. This resulted in the single bloodiest day in the history of the nation. Although Lee remained in place immediately after the battle, he quickly retreated to Virginia. This victory gave Lincoln the strength to issue the Preliminary Emancipation Proclamation.[3]

Highly annoyed at McClellan for his failure to pursue Lee after the Battle of Antietam, Lincoln appointed Maj. Gen. Ambrose E. Burnside commander of the Army of the Potomac. Burnside marched his army to Fredericksburg, Virginia. However, pontoons necessary to cross the Rappahannock River had not arrived. This gave Lee time to reposition his army on the high ground behind the city, especially along a portion labeled Marye's Heights that included the Sunken Road. In spite of the obvious disadvantage to his men, on December 13, Burnside ordered a series of assaults against the well-protected rebels. The result was almost 13,000 Federal casualties and a resounding Union defeat. Further attempts at maneuvering resulted in the infamous Mud March leading to Burnside's removal.[4]

In May 1863 Lincoln's new commander, Maj. Gen. Joseph Hooker, advanced his Army of the Potomac toward Richmond. In perhaps Lee's finest hour, he split his Army of Northern Virginia near Chancellorsville, sending Lieut. Gen. Thomas J. "Stonewall" Jackson of First Manassas fame on a great flanking maneuver that decisively defeated Hooker. While Hooker retreated, Lee advanced.[5]

Taking advantage of this momentum, Lee then invaded Pennsylvania. After maneuvering to confuse the new Union commander of the Army of the Potomac, Maj. Gen. George G. Meade, the armies collided at the small town of Gettysburg, Pennsylvania. During the first three days of July, the most famous battle of the war took place. Lee went on the offensive all three days, but after the infamous Pickett-Pettigrew-Trimble Charge failed on the third day, he suffered a major defeat. The Confederate commander retreated to Virginia, now forced to remain on the defensive.[6]

Lincoln finally recognized the need for a qualified general to take over from the bureaucrat Maj. Gen. Henry Halleck as general-in-chief of the Union armies. Therefore, the president appointed Maj. Gen. Ulysses S. Grant lieutenant general in March 1864. This appointment followed that officer's many successes in the Western Theater, which we will review next. Grant decided to assume overall command from the Eastern Theater while accompanying Meade in an "advisory" role. Following Grant's guidance, Meade instigated the Battles of the Wilderness and Spotsylvania Court House in May, resulting in huge casualties.[7]

After these battles Grant confronted Lee again at Cold Harbor ordering an assault resulting in the loss of some seven thousand Yankees. He then maneuvered around Lee and confronted him at Petersburg. Unwilling to order more direct assaults, he established a siege line east and south of that city which Lee would manage to resist for the rest of the year and into the following spring.[8]

Turning to events in the Western Theater, generally consisting of the area west of the Appalachian Mountains, the Union forces made significantly better progress.

Confederate president Jefferson Davis appointed fellow West Point classmate Leonidas Polk major general and temporary commander of essentially the entire Western Theater. Desiring Columbus, Kentucky, a prime defensive location on the Mississippi River, Polk violated that commonwealth's strict policy of neutrality by seizing the city on September 4, 1861. Grant immediately captured Paducah, Kentucky. On November 7 he moved down the Mississippi and attacked the small rebel camp at Belmont, Missouri, directly across the river and west of Columbus. Polk sent reinforcements and chased the Union commander back to his boats. While very small, the Battle of Belmont signaled that Grant was willing to fight.[9]

In February 1862 Grant received permission to capture Fort Henry guarding the Tennessee River, an excellent avenue deep into the western Confederacy. Working with the navy, he quickly did so. He then advanced to Fort Donelson guarding the Cumberland River, which flowed past the Confederate capital of Nashville. After some tough fighting, the rebel command unconditionally surrendered some thirteen thousand troops to "Unconditional Surrender" Grant, whose new nickname matched his initials.[10]

In preparation for advancing on and capturing the very important railroad crossing at Corinth, Mississippi, Grant moved up the Tennessee River (traveling south) and established a camp at Pittsburg Landing, near the small Shiloh Church. While awaiting reinforcements from Maj. Gen. Don C. Buell's Army of the Ohio, rebels under the command of Gen. Albert S. Johnston cobbled together a makeshift army and attacked early on the morning of April 6. Quickly disorganized, the Confederate army nonetheless pushed the Union line back toward the landing. During afternoon combat, Johnston

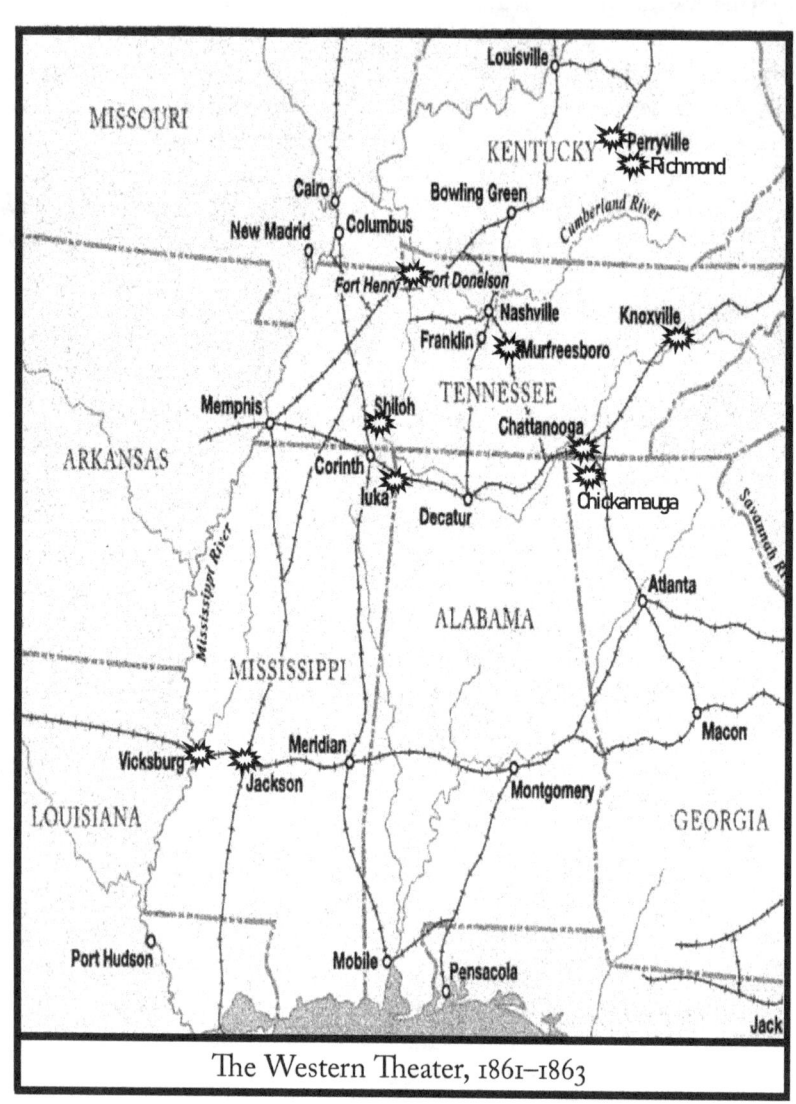
The Western Theater, 1861–1863

died from a wound he discovered too late. Assuming command, Gen. P. G. T. Beauregard called off the fighting in the late afternoon, with the rebels sure of victory the following day. Unfortunately for them, Grant was heavily reinforced overnight, and he attacked the Confederate army, eventually driving it from the field. The Battle of Shiloh was the bloodiest battle so far, indicating that the war would not likely end anytime soon.[11]

Department commander Maj. Gen. Henry W. Halleck assumed overall command, combined his armies, and slowly advanced on Corinth. As Halleck's force was twice the size of his own, Beauregard surreptitiously yielded the city to the Yankees and retreated fifty miles south to Tupelo, Mississippi. There he temporarily left the army to regain his health. Not a fan of the Creole general, President Davis quickly appointed second-in-command Gen. Braxton Bragg the new commander of what eventually was named the Army of Tennessee. Bragg went to work rebuilding his force.[12]

Meanwhile, Maj. Gen. Edmund Kirby Smith, a hero of the Battle of First Manassas, sought help to defend his Department of East Tennessee from portions of Halleck's force advancing on Chattanooga, a vital rebel railroad junction with lines converging from all directions. He convinced Bragg to provide help, and that officer eventually transferred most of his force to the city. The two generals agreed that Kirby Smith would first capture Cumberland Gap at the east end of his department, and then the two commands would jointly advance north into Tennessee and Kentucky. However, enamored with indications that Kentucky was ready for Confederate occupation, Kirby Smith bypassed the gap and advanced on his own into the commonwealth. On August 30 he won a decisive victory, the most one-sided of the war, at Richmond, Kentucky, and then captured Lexington and the capital city of Frankfort.[13]

Bragg, who ranked higher that Kirby Smith, had not realized that the latter commanded his own department and was not his subordinate. Kirby Smith relished independent command and remained in Kentucky, avoiding Bragg as long as possible. Bragg initially advanced toward Nashville but decided to continue into Kentucky. He avoided confronting Buell's army, allowing that general to retreat with his men to their base at Louisville. Bragg finally caught up with Kirby Smith and assumed overall command while his army marched northeast.[14]

Buell quickly reorganized and refitted his Army of the Ohio and advanced east on October 1 to confront Bragg's forces. One of the rebel commander's corps stopped in Perryville to confront the advance of Buell's army. Bragg ordered additional forces to assist, charging Polk with managing the attack. Hearing no firing on October 8 as ordered, Bragg rode to Perryville. Polk had held a council of war, and the commanders collectively decided to maintain the "offensive-defensive"—in other words, to see what developed. Furious at Polk's disobedience, the Confederate commander revised his line and then ordered an assault on what turned out to be Buell's First Corps, just arriving on the Mackville Road. Fearing he didn't have the rest of his corps in position, Buell postponed his planned attack on what he thought was the entire Confederate army until the next day. Bragg's small force drove the First Corps back almost a mile, scoring a tactical victory at the Battle of Perryville.[15]

Due to the prevailing drought, the shortage of supplies, and, most importantly, the failure of Kentucky men to enlist in his army, Bragg ordered both his and Kirby Smith's armies to retreat back to Tennessee. Buell declined to pursue owing to the lack of available forage and supplies. After an arduous march back into that state, the Confederate commander positioned his army around Murfreesboro, spread out for forage, assuming the fighting was over until spring because of the often-terrible conditions of the roads.[16]

For failing to pursue the rebel armies, the Lincoln administration immediately replaced Buell with Maj. Gen. William S. Rosecrans. The president and his staff also ordered an immediate attack on the Confederates around Murfreesboro. Stalling for time while rebuilding his army, "Rosey" maneuvered his three wings toward Murfreesboro the day after Christmas. Caught by surprise, Bragg recalled his units and positioned them on both sides of Stones River near that city. By the evening of December 30, the armies confronted each other.[17]

Both commanders planned to initiate battle early the next morning by rolling up the right flank of their opponent. Because the Confederates were not allowed to have fires as the lines were so close, they were ready to attack earlier, and they quickly caught the Union army's right wing by surprise. The rebels continued their assault and drove the Yankees back, almost severing their supply line. Exhausted and sustaining large numbers of casualties, the fighting finally sputtered to a halt with the Federal army located near and around the Round Forest, a slight elevation by the Murfreesboro Road and the railroad. Both sides expected fighting on New Year's Day, but little occurred. On January 2, Bragg, fearing problems on his right flank, ordered Confederates to assault the Union left to prevent its capture of higher ground. The last-minute placement of some fifty Federal cannon defending McFadden's Ford completely ruined the rebel offensive, resulting in significant casualties.[18]

After five nights in subfreezing weather, and with Stones River rising and threatening to separate his command, Bragg retreated south into the Tennessee highlands. Abandoning the field finally provided the Union with

Introduction

a victory at the Battle of Stones River, or Murfreesboro. This triumph gave President Lincoln enough potency to issue the Emancipation Proclamation, officially in force on January 1, 1863, and free (in theory) those slaves within Confederate-held territory. Both armies spent the rest of the winter and spring refitting.[19]

Beginning in late 1862, Grant had focused on capturing Vicksburg, the last major impediment to the opening of the Mississippi River to Federal river traffic, and on severing one-third of the Confederacy from the rest of the seceded states. After a series of failures, in the late spring of 1863, he marched his command down the west side of the river past his target city. The navy then successfully ran past the rebel defenses. With the navy's help Grant crossed the river, and instead of immediately advancing to Vicksburg, he waged a brilliant campaign in which he fought his way to and captured the Mississippi state capital of Jackson. After destroying military stores there, the Federal commander maneuvered west, cutting the railroad supply line to Vicksburg and fighting battles at Champion Hill and Big Black River Bridge. The Confederates fell back into the defenses at that city. Grant ordered assaults twice against the well-established rebel fortifications, but these were unsuccessful. He then laid siege to the impoverished bastion. Finally, on July 3, the Confederates showed the white flag, and Grant and commander Lieut. Gen. John Pemberton arranged the surrender details. Coincidentally, on July 4, Independence Day, the Union army marched into Vicksburg, allowing the Mississippi River to flow "again . . . unvexed to the sea," as Lincoln described it.[20]

The Union victory at Gettysburg and the capture of Vicksburg and the resulting opening of the Mississippi River for Union commerce captured the attention of citizens on both sides on the fighting. Yet a lesser-known third campaign had very consequential results. After reorganizing and refitting all winter and spring, Rosecrans finally unleashed his army. Bragg's troops were spread out some seventy miles along the Highland Rim in Tennessee to gain the most forage possible. The Union commander took advantage of the enemy's dispersed army—beginning on June 24, in nine days and at the cost of six hundred casualties, Rosecrans quickly outflanked the rebels, forcing Bragg to retreat all the way to Chattanooga. Often overshadowed, the Tullahoma Campaign was a brilliant maneuver that produced tangible results.[21]

Once again, Rosecrans paused to refit and resupply. Beginning on August 16, he sent three of his four corps to the Tennessee River and then across it. Maneuvering separately, these units marched over the mountains south of Chattanooga and soon dispersed over forty miles. Rosecrans abruptly realized that each corps was now exposed and could possibly be pounced on by Bragg. The Confederate commander abandoned the vital railroad center and made several attempts to do just that, but he was thwarted by subordinate commanders. Fearing retribution, these officers failed to carry out Bragg's orders to assault the Union force in McLemore's Cove, a valley south of Chattanooga. Rosey ordered his corps to reunite and maneuver back to their new supply base at Chattanooga.[22]

General Bragg then recognized he might block Rosecrans from arriving at his supply base and made plans to do exactly that. Meanwhile, discussion by the Confederate high command resulted in the transfer of two divisions of Lee's army commanded by Lieut. Gen. James Longstreet to augment Bragg's troops. Bragg began maneuvering his army south of Chattanooga, crossing Chickamauga Creek to confront the now-combined Union army. However, the Yankees were closer to Chattanooga than Bragg realized. The forces made initial contact on September 18, but the main fighting began the next morning.[23]

Discovering unexpected Yankees at Reed's Bridge over Chickamauga Creek, both sides sent reinforcements. The Battle of Chickamauga then began in earnest. Federals and rebels threw in division after division over the length of several miles, often fighting in timber with much-reduced visibility. The day's combat culminated with a very unusual Confederate night assault that quickly ground to a halt. Bragg issued orders for an early morning assault on the north end of Rosecrans's line which extended along the LaFayette Road. Late that evening Longstreet arrived with several of his brigades. Finding Bragg's headquarters, the commanding general immediately reorganized his army into two wings, with Longstreet now in command of the left wing![24]

The Battle of Chickamauga continued the next day, but not as Bragg had ordered. There was no early morning assault. The rebel commander's orders were not passed on as they should have been, and when he visited the right wing, many soldiers were eating breakfast. This failure allowed the Union army to continue to build and reinforce fortifications. When the right wing's assault finally occurred, after some success, it was repulsed. However, due perhaps to the fog of battle, the rebel cause took a turn for the better. In one of the quirks of battle, Rosecrans incorrectly believed that a hole in his line needed to be filled. Therefore, he pulled a division out of the line, inadvertently opening a significant gap. Longstreet had lined up his left wing in a column of divisions and brigades and was ready to attack as soon as he heard the right wing begin its action. Around 11:30 a.m. he ordered the assault, which quickly advanced west across the LaFayette Road at the Yankee line. Fortuitously for the Confederates, Longstreet's assault went directly through the aforementioned gap, dividing the Union army and easily routing a good part of it. While victory was all but ensured, Union corps commander Maj. Gen. George H.

Thomas managed to round up enough troops to hold off rebel assaults on the north end of the battlefield dubbed Horseshoe Ridge. With some additional reinforcements, Thomas's efforts allowed the rest of Rosecrans's army to escape to Chattanooga, at which point he skillfully withdrew. For his endeavors Thomas earned the sobriquet "the Rock of Chickamauga."[25]

The Battle of Chickamauga was the Army of Tennessee's one major victory during its existence. Unfortunately, Bragg failed to pursue the fleeing Yankees into Chattanooga, the Federal goal all along, and the win was largely wasted. The rebel commander established a semi siege around the city, causing a terrible reduction in supplies. Meanwhile, Grant was appointed commander of the new Military Division of the Mississippi, consisting of the Departments of the Cumberland, Ohio, and Tennessee, and he replaced Rosecrans with Thomas. Arriving at Chattanooga, Grant established an ingenious line of supply, the Cracker Line, and brought in further reinforcements in addition to those sent by Lincoln.[26]

Rather than concentrate on the Union force in Chattanooga, Bragg focused on eliminating some of his recalcitrant generals. He actually reduced the size of his command by sending Longstreet, who coveted army command, to Knoxville. Bragg believed that his line along Missionary Ridge southeast of the city, which continued west across Lookout Mountain, was simply invincible. Grant saw the terrain differently.[27]

Reinforced with his old army, the Army of the Tennessee, now led by Maj. Gen. William T. Sherman, the Union commander ordered Sherman to advance southeast along the crest of Missionary Ridge and roll up the rebel line. In position on November 24, Sherman discovered that he and his men faced a heretofore-unknown gap in the ridge, which was defended on the other side by a Confederate force. Meanwhile, another part of Grant's command under Maj. Gen. Joseph Hooker successfully captured Lookout Mountain by early the next day. With Sherman stalled, Grant ordered Thomas's army to conduct a demonstration or diversionary movement to the base of Missionary Ridge and possibly remove some of the pressure on Sherman. However, upon reaching the base, the Yankees found themselves in an untenable position: they were being fired on from above and laterally, and retreat would expose them to being shot in the back. Though unauthorized, Thomas's command nonetheless began ascending the ridge. Since the Confederate line ran along the topographical crest, not the military crest (see the discussion of crests in chapter 1), some cover was available to Thomas's men. Once atop the ridge, the Federal soldiers quickly overran the rebels, routing them. Although events had not been planned this way, Grant earned a decisive victory and freed Chattanooga from Confederate control.[28]

The totally demoralized rebels retreated south to Dalton, Georgia, where they established winter quarters. Bragg offered his resignation, which was immediately accepted. President Davis replaced him with Gen. Joseph E. Johnston, who ordered fortifications built to defend Dalton, and did his best to resupply and refit his beleaguered army. The Union force remained in and around Chattanooga for the winter.[29]

President Lincoln initially maintained his designated role as commander in chief. He eventually appointed Halleck as general-in-chief, but that general was more of a clerk than a commander. Lincoln finally decided that he needed a leader who might oversee the combined operations and armies of the Union. Having successfully won three campaigns, Grant was the obvious choice. On February 29, 1864, the president signed into law the bill Congress had passed establishing the grade of lieutenant general. The lieutenant general selectee made his way to Washington, DC, where he was formally promoted on March 9 and also met Lincoln for the first time. This promotion would have a very direct effect on the Union conduct of the war for 1864.[30]

Grant made the momentous decision to go east and "advise" Meade, the commander of the Army of the Potomac, on how to conduct that force. He selected Sherman to replace himself as commander of the Military Division of the Mississippi. In this role, Sherman would then oversee what today is defined as an army group, consisting of three armies. As we shall see, Sherman was a much less aggressive commander than Grant, and this attitude might potentially have lengthened the war.[31]

Sherman concentrated his armies around Chattanooga and prepared for the upcoming campaign. His orders from Grant were to move against Johnston's army concentrated at Dalton. The Union commander worked hard to make his supply line, the Western and Atlantic Railroad, capable of handling the huge amount of foodstuffs, ammunition, and other items necessary to adequately support his force.[32]

What would be quickly labeled the Atlanta Campaign began on May 7, 1864. Taking advantage of the natural defense provided by Rocky Face Ridge surrounding Dalton, Johnston had erected additional fortifications. Rather than going on the offensive as the Confederate government desired, he awaited Sherman's attack. While Sherman faced the north and west sides of the city, he had no intention of ordering any major assaults, as they would be too costly in terms of casualties. He instead directed a few token assaults while preparing a turning maneuver.[33]

In February scouts informed Thomas that Snake Creek Gap, located about twelve miles south of Dalton, provided access for a turning movement and was unmonitored by the rebels. Sherman ordered Maj. Gen. James B. McPherson

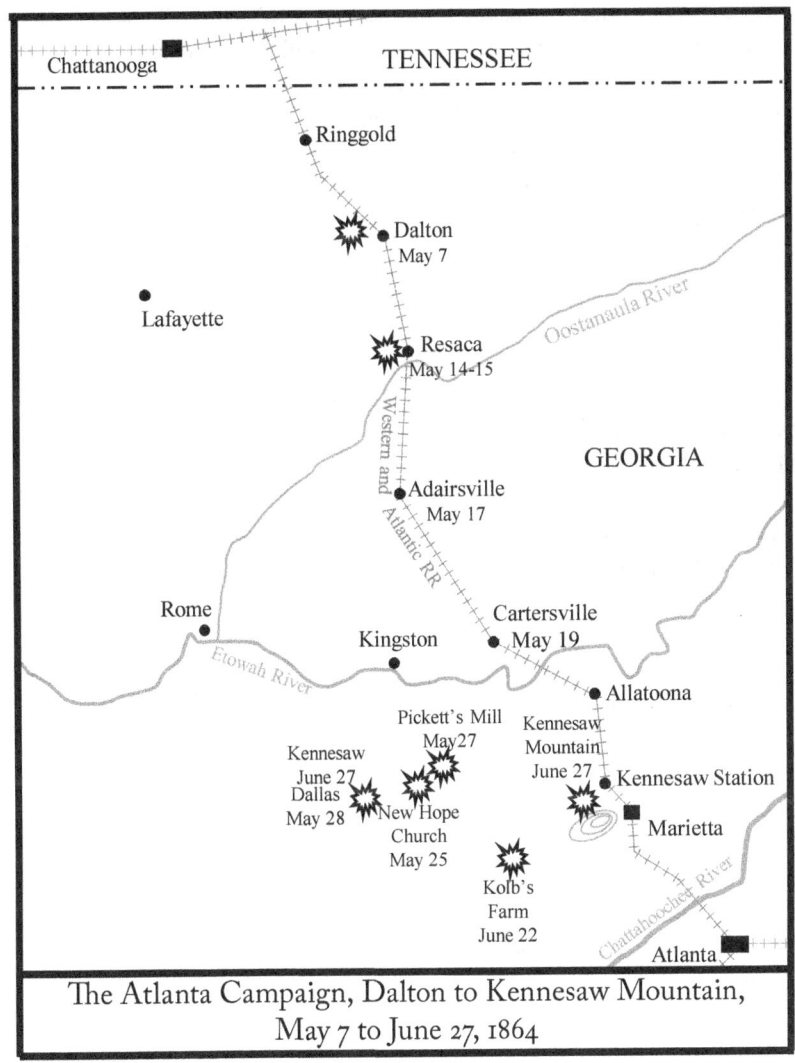

The Atlanta Campaign, Dalton to Kennesaw Mountain, May 7 to June 27, 1864

and his Army of the Tennessee to march via Villanow to the gap, then continue east to the small town of Resaca located on the Western and Atlantic Railroad. If McPherson was able to sever the railroad there, Johnston's supply line would be cut, forcing him out of Dalton. It was a brilliant plan. Unfortunately, when the Union general reached Resaca, he was confronted by a small force of Confederates. Overestimating the size of this command and fearing he was too vulnerable to attack by Johnston, McPherson quickly retreated to the gap. Sherman commented to him a few days later, "Well Mac, you have missed the opportunity of a lifetime." Sherman then brought the rest of his command through the gap and approached Resaca.[34]

Johnston immediately reacted, sending his army to Resaca; the troops arrived just ahead of the combined Union force. On May 14 the Battle of Resaca commenced with small assaults by both sides. While the Union commander watched these attacks, he had another plan. He ordered a division to cross the Oostanaula River downstream in an attempt to outflank the rebels. Met by a Confederate force that Bragg had positioned near Calhoun for observation, the Yankees retreated. While the battle continued the next day, Sherman sent the same division back across the river, and this time it successfully remained. Additionally, some of the Federals managed to capture a hill west of the town and quickly place artillery on it. These guns had the range of both the road and railroad bridges crossing the Oostanaula River, Johnston's logical line of retreat. Therefore, he ordered that retreat on the night of the fifteenth, conducting it successfully.[35]

After an attempt to ambush part of the Union force near Cassville on May 19, Bragg continued retreating across the Etowah River to Allatoona Pass. The railroad cut through the Allatoona Mountains there, providing the Confederates a very strong defensive position. As the Union commander was familiar with the terrain from passing through the area years before the war, he knew it would be extremely costly in terms of casualties to try and assault that position. While his men were given a few days' rest, Sherman devised another plan.[36]

He concluded that the best course of action was to make a wheeling movement to the west, leaving the vital railroad line of supply. However, when the movement commenced, Sherman discovered that the Confederate army had also shifted to confront the Yankees. Underestimating the strength of the enemy force facing him, on May 25 Sherman ordered an attack on the new rebel line at New Hope Church. Conducted in a driving thunderstorm, the attack failed. After stretching his line all the way west to Dallas, Sherman recognized that his maneuvering hadn't fooled Johnston, so he ordered part of his force back toward the railroad. The Confederates were able to temporarily halt the Federals at the Battle of Pickett's Mill on the twenty-seventh, inflicting some fifteen hundred casualties on that force. Nonetheless, the Yankee command was finally able to return to the railroad south of the pass, avoiding a confrontation there. Soldiers on both sides were glad to be away from what was immediately dubbed the Hell Hole.[37]

Johnston established what would be called the first of the mountain lines. It ran from Lost Mountain east of Dallas northeast to Pine Mountain, then continued across the railroad north of Marietta to Brushy Mountain. After refitting for a few days, Sherman's armies advanced down the Sandtown Road only to stumble on the new rebel line. Pine Mountain provided an excellent location for observation, but it required a salient in the Confederate line. Concerned about its vulnerability, Johnston and his corps commanders Lieut. Gen. William J. Hardee and Lieut. Gen. Leonidas Polk visited the summit on the morning of June 14. Sherman noticed the small group and ordered artillery fire on it, killing Polk. The Confederates abandoned Pine Mountain that evening.[38]

After his left was flanked, on the sixteenth Johnston withdrew this part of his force east across Mud Creek, now manning the Mud Creek Line. However, this line had another salient in it, forcing Johnston to retreat once again. This is where our text begins.[39]

CHAPTER 1

BEFORE THE BATTLE OF KENNESAW MOUNTAIN
JUNE 14–26, 1864

If you have bypassed the preface, please direct your attention there. Read the definition of a critical decision in order to understand more fully what this book discusses, and what it does and does not provide.

Prior to the small Battle of Kolb's Farm and the Battle of Kennesaw Mountain, five critical decisions ultimately resulted in the latter engagement, an important part of the Atlanta Campaign.

Johnston Abandons the Mud Creek Line and Retreats to the Kennesaw Mountain Line

Situation

As described in the introduction, Gen. Joseph E. Johnston ordered a series of retreats from his Army of Tennessee's winter location in and around Dalton. He did so in response to Maj. Gen. William T. Sherman's aggressive flanking movements. Johnston established his Mud Creek Line, his seventh defensive line since the campaign began, on June 17. Due to pressure on his left in the area surrounding the Gilgal Church, he refused his left beginning on the night of June 16. Abandoning the original line from Lost Mountain

Gen. Joseph E. Johnston, CSA.
Library of Congress.

past the important crossroads near the Gilgal Church, Johnston fell back to Mud Creek, which ran north to south rather than east to west. Mud Creek was about four miles distant from Kennesaw Mountain. Johnston ordered a new line dug behind (east of) the creek. His right remained in position from south of Pine Mountain running northeast to Brushy Mountain.[1]

Virginian Joseph Eggleston Johnston, a classmate of Robert E. Lee's, graduated from West Point in 1829. Appointed quartermaster general with the rank of brigadier general in 1860, he resigned and obtained a commission as brigadier general in the Regular Army of the Confederacy in May 1861. Eventually Confederate president Jefferson Davis appointed him one of five initial full generals to rank from July 4, 1861. Believing he outranked the other four, including Lee, Johnston began a continuously negative relationship with Davis. Abhorring failure, Johnston consistently refused to go on the offensive. As a result, during the Atlanta Campaign he constantly retreated, much to the consternation of the Confederacy. Although Johnston strove to take care of his men, they eventually became concerned with the constant withdrawing.[2]

The problem with the Mud Creek Line was that it angled sharply in the center, abruptly turning from a southwest direction from Brushy Mountain near the Latimer House, then extending directly south to around the Marietta–Dallas Road. This resulted in a salient, or significant bend, in the

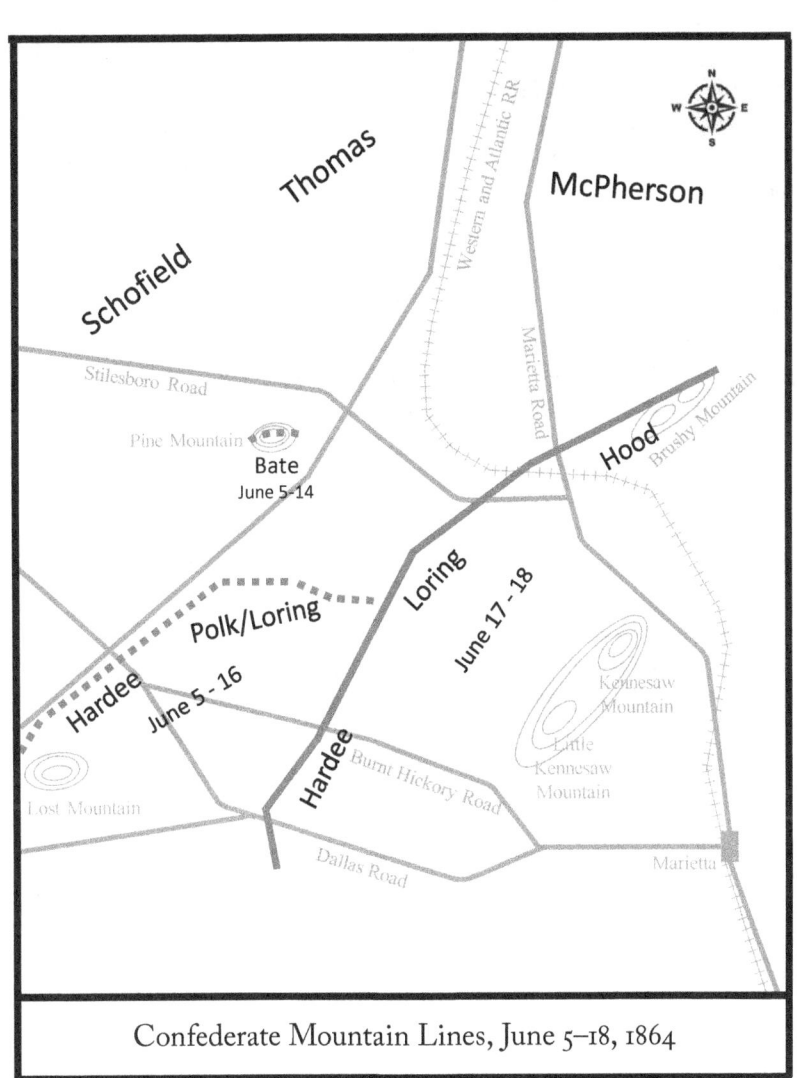

Confederate Mountain Lines, June 5–18, 1864

line that Johnston must defend. Exposed on the front as well as parts of both sides, salients are particularly vulnerable to enemy fire and harder to protect. Johnston knew he would have a difficult time defending this new line from Sherman.[3]

Options

Johnston quickly realized that he would not be able to adequately defend his new Mud Creek Line due to the exposed salient. He had two options. He could re-form the Mud Creek Line by eliminating the salient, or he could retreat.[4]

Option 1

Johnston might designate a change in his line that eliminated the vulnerable salient. However, this realignment would require construction while under fire by Maj. Gen. William T. Sherman's opposing force. The terrain present offered no significant realignment possibilities.[5]

Option 2

The rebel commander was quite aware that only a few miles away a natural, very imposing defensive line had already been under construction since June 17. This line lay on Big and Little Kennesaw Mountains northwest of Marietta, and it continued south on what eventually was labeled Pigeon Hill, crossing the Marietta–Dallas Road to Kolb's Farm. This line's favorable defensive strength would provide Johnston with a much better position versus Sherman.[6]

Decision

General Johnston quickly decided to retreat to what would be designated as the Kennesaw Mountain Line, his eighth defensive position since the beginning of the Atlanta Campaign.[7]

Results/Impact

Johnston's decision to retreat to the formidable Kennesaw Mountain Line determined the location for the upcoming Battle of Kennesaw Mountain. He positioned his three corps along this new line. Hood's Corps initially held the ground from Brushy Mountain north of Kennesaw Mountain curving southwest across the Western and Atlantic Railroad, toward that mountain. Maj. Gen. William W. Loring, temporarily in command of Polk's Corps

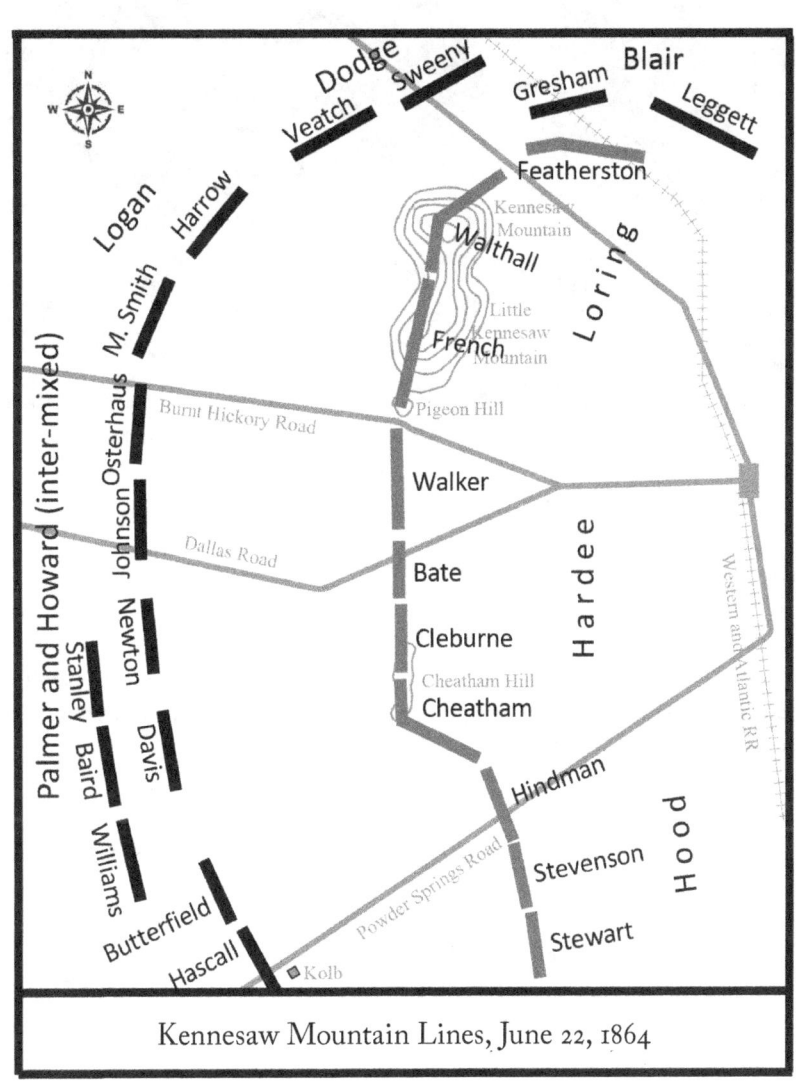
Kennesaw Mountain Lines, June 22, 1864

Big and Little Kennesaw Mountains, near Marietta, GA. *Photographic History of the Civil War*, Vol. III, 127.

following his death, continued the line south past Little Kennesaw Mountain to a smaller eminence, referred to as Kennesaw Spur. The spur was designated Pigeon Hill long after the war, apparently due to passenger pigeons passing through on the eastern flyway, and I will continue that trend since virtually all sources and maps label it as such. Hardee's Corps covered the ground south of Pigeon Hill, crossing the road from Marietta to Dallas, stretching south past another hill that would soon be dubbed Cheatham Hill, and extending almost to the Powder Springs Road. However, as we will see, Johnston would soon amend his line.[8]

The rebel soldiers quickly heavily fortified this new line, established earlier by Johnston's chief engineer, Lieut. Col. Stephen W. Presstman, building strong trenches secured with head logs and placing abatis in front of them where possible. Rain continued to hamper operations on both sides. The Kennesaw Mountain Line extended some seven miles in length. At this stage of the war, Federals and rebels knew that a properly built, heavily manned defensive line was almost impossible to overrun by assault. Hence all soldiers, anytime a halt of more than just a few hours occurred, learned to immediately build defensive works. Within twenty-four hours troops would complete almost impregnable defensive works, only to continue to do so at their next stop.[9]

Maj. Gen. William T. Sherman, USA.
Library of Congress.

In response to the Confederates' retreat several miles to the Kennesaw Mountain Line, Sherman quickly followed Johnston and positioned his seven corps opposite it. At the same time, the Union commander debated what his next movement should be. Maj. Gen. James B. McPherson's Army of the Tennessee dug in opposite the northern end of Johnston's line, while Maj. Gen. George H. Thomas's Army of the Cumberland, specifically the Fourth and Fourteenth Corps, manned the center. Hooker's Twentieth Corps and Maj. Gen. John M. Schofield's Army of the Ohio (essentially the Twenty-Third Corps) confronted the southern segment of the rebel commander's line and more. The Union line, by necessity, stretched over ten miles in length.[10]

Johnston's Kennesaw Mountain Line would be his best defensive position of this portion of the Atlanta Campaign. Sherman conceded that the rebel position was "unusually strong." However, as Richard McMurry so succinctly comments, if Johnston failed to conduct an active defense, it would simply be a matter of time and favorable weather before Sherman resorted to another flanking maneuver.[11]

Cheatham Decides to Defend a Salient in the Kennesaw Mountain Line

The Confederates had begun work on the Kennesaw Mountain Line on June 17 prior to occupying it on the nineteenth. That evening, Major Presstman and his engineers laid out the actual line to be defended. As one can imagine, doing so in the dark hampered their ability to accurately find the best location for the line, which covered many miles. While the site generally was so logical that any veteran private could establish it, there were certainly some exceptions. The key exception was at what would quickly be dubbed Cheatham Hill.[12]

This hill was located a mile or so south of the Marietta–Dallas Road and had a commanding, dominating view of the terrain to the west of it. However, daylight exposed the obvious danger of this salient and the difficulty involved in defending it. Salients exposed the troops guarding them to enemy fire not only in the front but also along the sides. The only possible advantage of a salient is that it can allow its defenders to provide enfilading fire if other points along the attached line are assaulted. This salient immediately attracted the attention of the Federals, who quickly fired on it with artillery. Maj. Gen. Benjamin F. "Frank" Cheatham, whose division was tasked with defending part of the Kennesaw Mountain Line including this hill, had a serious problem to deal with at this location.[13]

A native Tennessean, Cheatham served in the Mexican-American War as a colonel commanding the Tennessee Volunteers. After a brief sojourn to the gold fields of California, Frank returned to Tennessee and engaged in farming while simultaneously attaining the rank of major general command-

The Dead Angle, Cheatham Hill, Kennesaw Mountain National Battlefield Park. Photo by the author.

June 14–26, 1864

Maj. Gen. Benjamin F. Cheatham, CSA. Library of Congress.

ing the state militia. The Confederacy appointed him brigadier general on July 9, 1861, and major general from March 10, 1862. Cheatham was a "good old boy" beloved by the Tennesseans whom he commanded. In addition to a fondness for horses, he loved the bottle. Gen. Braxton Bragg accused him of being drunk during the Battle of Stones River. Bragg and Cheatham despised each other, but Frank was an excellent commander, leading a brigade, division, and eventually a corps in almost every engagement fought by the Army of Tennessee.[14]

Options

Cheatham needed to quickly determine whether to accept the line around the salient as it had just been laid out, or to designate a new line better suited for defense of the hill that would soon bear his name.[15]

Option 1

The easiest option for Cheatham would be to accept the designated line and heavily fortify it. The general knew that this position commanded immediate Federal attention, and it was more vulnerable than virtually any other along the Kennesaw Mountain Line. Because of the terrain, he realized that moving slightly back to another location would not greatly enhance troops' defensive ability. With extensive building, Cheatham's men might perhaps erect an impregnable line of defense at the established line.[16]

Option 2

By retiring his line some distance from the originally designated one, Cheatham might somewhat reduce his soldiers' exposure. Realistically, however, the terrain immediately behind the initial line was not much more favorable, and it would only increase the rebels' inability to view an enemy assault (due to the merits of a topographical crest versus a military crest, which will be discussed in relation to the next critical decision). This location was the only real weakness in the otherwise highly defensible Kennesaw Mountain Line.[17]

Decision

Frank Cheatham quickly decided to accept the designated position as it was and heavily fortify it. Although Johnston and his command initially could not be assured, this site would become the focus of the upcoming Battle of Kennesaw Mountain and strongly influence the outcome of the fighting and subsequent events, as we will see.[18]

Results/Impact

Cheatham's acceptance of the line on the salient resulted in his division, especially that part stationed on the salient, receiving a direct assault by many units of Sherman's combined armies, the main component or focus of the Battle of Kennesaw Mountain. However, we don't want to get ahead of ourselves. The following critical decision ties in very directly with this one, further complicating the Confederate defenses.[19]

Confederate Engineers Use the Topographical Crest Instead of the Military Crest

Situation

The type of line Johnston's engineers laid out compounded Cheatham's problem defending the salient on soon-to-be-named Cheatham Hill.[20]

Options

By this time in the war, army engineers, not to mention veteran privates, used one of two types of lines: those conforming to the topographical crest or to

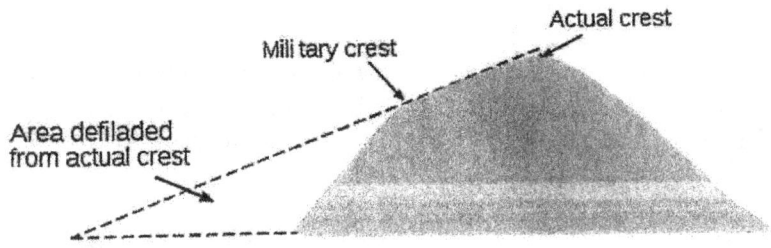

Military crest versus topographical crest. AR- 310-25, *Dictionary of United States Army Terms,* October 15, 1983, 117.

the military crest. On the Kennesaw Mountain Line Johnston's engineers had their choice, subject to the whim of the commander, to use either.[21]

Option 1

Confederate engineers could lay the Kennesaw Mountain Line along the topographical crest running along a ridge's highest points. For the rebels, one advantage of a line along a topographical crest was that enemy troops would commonly overshoot it. Yet while this choice was seemingly a logical one for Johnston's engineers, it would have disadvantages. It would allow troops, cannon, and fortifications to be outlined against the sky, providing easy targets for the enemy. Other more significant problems included the fact that a topographical crest might not provide the best view of the attacking enemy, nor would it allow for the best fields of fire.[22]

Option 2

The Kennesaw Mountain Line could also be laid along the military crest. A military crest is defined as "a fixed line on the forward slope of a hill or ridge from which maximum observation covering the slope down to the base of the hill or ridge can be obtained." It is further defined as "an area on the forward or reverse slope of a hill or ridge just below the topographical crest from which maximum observation and direct fire covering the slope down to the base of the hill or ridge can be obtained." A line on the military crest would help the Confederates sooner observe movements of attacking enemy troops, but it would also allow maximum defensive firepower to bear on the Federals at the earliest opportunity.[23]

Decision

For unknown reasons, Johnston's engineers used the military crest along parts of the Kennesaw Mountain Line but reverted to the topographical crest at Cheatham Hill. Perhaps darkness can be blamed for the oversight. Nighttime only added to Cheatham's difficulties in defending the salient.[24]

Results/Impact

For reasons seemingly unexplained thus far, the Army of Tennessee desired to use the topographical crest. It had done so both at Chattanooga and up to this point in the Atlanta Campaign. Relating specifically to the salient at Cheatham Hill, this decision resulted in a much-limited field of fire for its defenders, specifically for the men of Brig. Gen. George E. Maney's and Brig. Gen. Alfred J. Vaughan Jr.'s brigades. The choice created some fifty-plus yards of dead ground where the rebels were unable to see and fire at Federals. While the salient was quickly named the Dead Angle for the carnage that resulted there, this name also describes an area where the defending brigades could not confront the enemy until they advanced quite close to the defenses.[25]

While the rebels nonetheless would successfully defend this salient, the reduced fields of fire would provide the Union assaulting force with an option not initially considered, as we will discuss in a following critical decision.[26]

Cheatham Carefully Locates and Camouflages His Artillery

Situation

Frank Cheatham knew that the salient on what would soon be dubbed Cheatham Hill and the Dead Angle would quickly attract the attention of the Union command, likely providing it as a natural target for assault because of its exposure. The Yankees confirmed Cheatham's thinking with artillery fire directed at it on the morning of June 21, undoubtedly hurrying up his decision to quickly fortify. By this time in the war, both sides automatically and immediately erected defensive structures anytime a halt of significance was made. Head logs and firing platforms were now incorporated into the defenses, along with abatis (pointed tree trucks) and chevaux-de-frise (strong pointed sticks). Federals and Confederates had learned the hard way that these updated defenses were virtually impregnable.[27]

Options

To assist in the defense of the salient, Cheatham had limited artillery available for counter–battery fire, as well as for anti–personnel fire in case of assault. At this stage of preparations, Cheatham had two options for his artillery. He could use it as counter–battery fire in reply to Union battery fire, or he could conceal it to make its presence a significant surprise complicating any Union assault on this position.[28]

Option 1

It would be natural for Cheatham, or any commander, to return fire when fired on. Doing so would tend to discourage enemy fire and encourage his troops to maintain their position. However, the Federals would be able to ascertain the location and likely number of guns and batteries the rebels possessed. Cheatham was well aware of this.[29]

Option 2

Were Cheatham to conceal his artillery and forbid its reply to Union fire, he would be able to provide strong additional firepower in case of enemy assault, as well as a surprise for the Yankees.[30]

Decision

The division commander camouflaged his artillery and forbade it from firing in order to maintain secrecy from the Union command. This decision ultimately provided significant additional firepower to the rebels and assisted in the firm repulse of the assault on June 27.[31]

Results/Impact

Cheatham methodically placed his artillery to defend the Dead Angle. He located the four 12-pound Napoleons of Phelan's Alabama Battery commanded by Lieut. Nathaniel Venable and the four guns of Capt. Thomas J. Perry's Florida Battery south of the salient. To provide cross fire, Cheatham positioned two more guns from Capt. John W. Mebane's Tennessee Battery, commanded by Lieut. Luke E. Wright, a hundred yards or so north of Vaughan's Brigade. Vaughan's men were defending the northern side of the salient.

These cannon greatly assisted in halting the Federal's assault on the Dead Angle on June 27, and they might likely have been the deciding factor in repulsing it.[32]

Why were these weapons so deadly? Canister fired from artillery at close range was extremely deadly, and a six-gun battery manned by veterans provided roughly the equivalent of an additional regiment's worth of fire. Canister usually contained twenty-seven balls weighing seven ounces each. These were packed in sawdust in four tiers within a can, and the can was attached to a sabot, or wood spacer. In turn, the sabot was attached to a powder charge. When fired the can would burst like a large shotgun, spewing the balls outward in a cone-shaped pattern. With a muzzle velocity of fifteen hundred feet per second (one thousand miles per hour), each ball had about fifteen times the stopping power of a one-ounce Minié ball. A veteran artillery crew could load and fire a gun three times per minute for a brief period of time. When the enemy got within two hundred yards or so of their position, the crew loaded double canister, removing the powder charge and placing an additional can of canister before the one with the charge. This literally doubled the outgoing balls. Six cannon firing almost fifty balls three times a minute, as was typical of a Union battery (rebel batteries usually contained four guns), equates to firing around one thousand balls per minute. This is the equivalent of a three-hundred-man regiment also firing three rounds per minute. Artillery were particularly deadly up close, and soldiers dreaded charging these weapons.[33]

Confederate Artillery Is Dragged to the Top of Big and Little Kennesaw Mountains

An integral part of any defensive line during the Civil War was artillery. We reviewed that concept at least somewhat in discussion of the preceding critical decision. Yet it appeared to many Confederates that parts of the newly manned Kennesaw Mountain Line would be devoid of artillery. Specifically, most rebels in these locations determined that it was impossible to position artillery on or near the summits of Kennesaw Mountain, rising some 679 feet above Marietta (1,129 feet above sea level) to 1,808 feet above sea level, and Little Kennesaw Mountain, ascending 481 feet above Marietta to 1,610 feet above sea level. The eminence labeled Pigeon Hill long after the war was 118 feet higher than Marietta at 1,247 feet above sea level. These heights were intimidating indeed to rebel artillerists. The Army of Tennessee's chief of artillery, Brig. Gen. Francis A. Shoup, considered it impossible to place artillery on these heights.[34]

The visibility from the tops of Big and Little Kennesaw Mountains was (and still is) spectacular and extremely valuable for military intelligence and operations. Yet the potential effect of locating artillery there was just as beneficial, for it could potentially dominate the area below within range.[35]

Options

Maj. George S. Storrs commanded Storrs's Artillery Battalion, which consisted of three batteries armed with ten Napoleons and two three-inch ordnance rifles, all attached to Maj. Gen. Samuel French's division of Loring's (formerly Polk's) Corps. Initially convinced of the impossibility of placing artillery on top of the two Kennesaw Mountains, he realized he faced two options. He could simply accept that it was impossible to locate his artillery on the high points, or he could attempt to do just that.[36]

Option 1

Storrs, like to his peers, could look for positions besides the peaks where his batteries would still be effective. This would be a very reasonable choice.[37]

Option 2

The major could give it a try and see whether, with enough help, he could engineer the hauling of at least some of his artillery to the tops of the mountains. This would require much-needed cooperation and manpower. If achieved, the placement of Storrs's artillery on top of Big and Little Kennesaw would provide excellent coverage for the line.[38]

Confederates dragging guns up Kennesaw Mountain. *Battles and Leaders*, Vol. 4, 271.

Decision

Storrs asked his division commander, French, for permission to try and drag his artillery up the mountains, and French ordered him to do so if possible.[39]

Results/Impact

With a lot of help, Major Storrs succeeded in bringing the artillery of his reserve, Capt. Henry Guibor's Missouri Battery and Capt. John J. Ward's Alabama Battery, plus Capt. James Hoskins's Mississippi Battery, and the Alabama Batteries of Capt. Richard H. Bellamy and Capt. Charles L. Lumsden, to the top of both mountains. He initially positioned nine guns on the relatively level summit of Little Kennesaw Mountain. Brig. Gen. Randall L. Gibson's brigade of Lieut. Gen. John B. Hood's corps was detailed to haul up ammunition as well as dig gun emplacements and parapets. Because of the uneven terrain at the peak of Kennesaw Mountain, fewer cannon were positioned there while the effort involved certainly contributed to that decision.[40]

These rebel cannon effectively controlled the Western and Atlantic Railroad as well as Sherman's possible approaches to Marietta and Atlanta from the northwest. This forced Sherman to rule out flanking Johnston on the Confederate right. However, the rebels on the tops of the two mountains quickly discovered the Union artillery could reach that high, forcing them to be diligent. Sherman would now consider flanking Johnston on his left, as he had typically been maneuvering in that direction. This development led to the next set of critical decisions.[41]

CHAPTER 2
THE BATTLE OF KOLB'S FARM
JUNE 21–22, 1864

Before the Battle of Kennesaw Mountain, Lieut. Gen. John B. Hood waged the much smaller Battle of Kolb's Farm, so named because of its location. Three critical decisions, one each by Maj. Gen. William T. Sherman, Gen. Joseph E. Johnston, and Hood, resulted in this action. Both sides suffered consequences from this fighting.

Sherman Attempts to Outflank Johnston's Left Flank

Situation

Sherman quickly realized that the Confederate Kennesaw Mountain Line was a superb defensive position. Initially, his best action was to avoid a confrontation there while he contemplated his options. He ordered skirmishing all along his lines in order to establish exactly where Johnston's new defensive line was located, and just how strong it appeared. Sherman had grown tired of the continuous flanking maneuvering since Johnston had refused to make a stand and attack the significantly larger Federal command. In fact, as noted above, this was Johnston's eighth fortified line since the campaign began.[1]

Johnston enjoyed two huge benefits while established on his Kennesaw Mountain Line. First, and most obviously, the line provided a superb defensive capability unequaled so far in the Atlanta Campaign. The second benefit was that the top of Kennesaw Mountain provided an excellent observation

The Battle of Kolb's Farm

platform for the rebels. At 1,808 feet above sea level, the mountain rises some 700 feet above the surrounding terrain. From atop it, rebel observers instantly viewed any and virtually all of the Federals' movements as they maneuvered in front of Johnston's Kennesaw Mountain Line. The only chance Sherman's various units had to maneuver in secret was at night or when the mountain top was hidden in clouds. Yet the next morning their new locations were generally obvious to the rebels.[2]

Options

As he and his men settled into their new positions as previously described, Sherman wrestled with what he should do next. The Kennesaw Mountain Line blocking his way forward initially appeared too formidable to assault directly. He could feel out Johnston's line by sending skirmishers forward all gauge rebel response, or he could try outflanking Johnston's left.[3]

Option 1

Rather than directly assault the rebel Kennesaw Mountain Line, Sherman could order skirmishers shaken out all along his own line to probe the Confederate formation for weakness. If this action determined few, if any, vulnerabilities in the Confederate force, the cost in casualties would likely remain low. With constant shifting a possibility within the rebel ranks, Sherman might discover a vulnerable location ripe for exploitation.[4]

Option 2

As Sherman had maneuvered continuously since the beginning of the campaign, he could potentially try and outflank Johnston's left. The Union commander mentioned this plan of maneuver in a letter to Lieut. Gen. Ulysses S. Grant dated April 10, 1864. With more troops, Sherman should be able to extend his right flank far enough to outstretch Johnston's line. He already had Hooker's and Schofield's corps moving in that direction. The advantage of this choice was that Sherman might possibly force Johnston to retreat again, with the Federals enduring few, if any, casualties.[5]

Decision

Sherman actually implemented both options. He used skirmishers to probe Johnston's line while ordering his own right flank to continue to advance southward. Sherman's right also attempted to maneuver around Johnston's left flank, guarded by Lieut. Gen. William J. Hardee's corps, south of the Dallas Road.[6]

June 21–22, 1864

Results/Impact

Skirmishing by Union forces failed to discover any apparent weakness in Johnston's line. Sherman ordered Maj. Gen. Joseph Hooker and his Twentieth Corps to shift south, while Maj. Gen. Oliver O. Howard's Fourth Corps replaced that force. The Federal commander ordered Maj. Gen. John M. Schofield's Army of the Ohio to extend as far south as possible to outflank Johnston. Schofield successfully maneuvered as ordered, and by the end of the day on June 20, he made his headquarters at the Andrew J. Cheney House, located on the Powder Springs Road. The next day Schofield continued maneuvering south and east while Hooker tried to maintain contact with Schofield's left flank. The results of this decision provided Sherman with enough information to eventually decide to assault Johnston's Kennesaw Mountain Line.[7]

As noted above, the rebels detected this attempt at outflanking their left. This caused Johnston to make the following critical decision, which in turn resulted in the Battle of Kolb's Farm.[8]

Johnston Orders Hood to Protect the Left Flank

Situation

The rebels atop Kennesaw Mountain discerned the movements to the south by Sherman's men. Johnston correctly feared that Sherman was attempting to outflank him to the south as he had previously continuously done. Johnston needed to formulate a solution to protect his left flank and hold Sherman back from further advancement into the interior of Georgia.[9]

Options

Johnston had two options to consider. He could order Hardee's Corps to move farther south and establish a new defensive line blocking Schofield and other Union elements. Alternatively, he could order another unit or units to occupy and continue the Confederate defensive line south of Hardee's present position.[10]

Option 1

Hardee's Corps was the nearest command to block Schofield and other Yankee units trying to position themselves to potentially outflank Johnston to the south. In a matter of hours Hardee could have his brigades relocate farther to the south to block any Union attempt to maneuver to the south and around

Johnston's new left flank. This option would provide the quickest response to Sherman's maneuvering.[11]

The disadvantage of this option was that Johnston would have to replace Hardee's Corps with parts of another corps, or with another entire corps. He needed to either shift his entire army to the south, backfilling the trenches and other defenses already established along the Kennesaw Mountain Line, or replace just Hardee. But pulling another corps or part of a corps out of the line to replace Hardee would, in and of itself, open another part of the line, which would require further backfilling by other units. Johnston's line was already stretched to the limit.[12]

Option 2

Johnston's other option was to essentially reposition his line by taking troops from his right flank. He assumed, based on the observations from Kennesaw Mountain and other reports from his cavalry, that Sherman's focus was the rebel left flank, not the right. More specifically, Johnston had the option of moving Lieut. Gen. John B. Hood's corps from his right flank to a new location connecting Hood's right flank to Hardee's left flank. This new position would also fill in a new line to the south, potentially blocking further Union maneuvering. In addition, it would provide a strong deterrent for Sherman's additional attempts to outflank Johnston. The Union commander's lines were even longer than Johnston's, and Sherman had a finite number of troops that he could only stretch so far.[13]

Two concerns would remain if Johnston chose this option. First, if he moved Hood's Corps from its location defending the right flank, Hood needed much more time to relocate his command. He and his men must march behind the Kennesaw Mountains, through Marietta, and back around to unite with Hardee. This journey would entail at least a full day's march. Could Hood arrive in time? Second, by shifting Hood from protecting the right flank, how could Johnston then defend that flank in case Sherman later attempted to advance around it?[14]

Decision

Johnston decided to protect his left and keep Sherman from further attempts to outflank him. To this end, Johnston ordered Hood to march his entire corps out from his position defending the right flank, continue through Marietta, and dig in to extend the Kennesaw Mountain Line south from Hardee's position. Perhaps another consideration in the rebel commander's decision was that he seemed to rely on Hood for the tougher assignments. Johnston gambled that Sherman would continue to fixate on maneuvering around the

June 21–22, 1864

left flank of the Confederate Kennesaw Mountain Line, ignoring the right flank. Confederate artillery on Kennesaw Mountain provided additional protection by covering the right flank. Johnston also ordered Maj. Gen. Joseph Wheeler's command to spread out and protect the vulnerable right flank to the best of its ability.[15]

Results/Impact

Hood pulled his corps out of its entrenchments on the Confederate right flank on June 21 and marched through Marietta as ordered. His corps encamped that night about two miles west of that city on the Powder Springs Road. The next morning Hood advanced generally along the Powder Springs Road to confront Sherman's units maneuvering on his right flank and hinder their further advancement. In the afternoon Hood began to align his corps with Hardee's. As described next, Hood also considered a reconnaissance to determine what Union commands were maneuvering in the area.[16]

In this series we don't consider simply reacting to a movement a critical decision. However, in this situation, Johnston's choice unknowingly resulted in the Battle of Kolb's Farm. If he had not placed Hood on his left flank in order to extend it, the following critical decision and resulting action would not have taken place in the form it did. Some other action or perhaps nonaction might have taken place, changing history on June 22. Therefore, Johnston's

Lieut. Gen. John B. Hood, CSA. *Photographic History of the Civil War*, Vol. 3, 123.

order for Hood to leave the rebel right flank and pass through Marietta was a critical decision. As we shall next see, Hood, of his own volition, ordered an engagement with the Federal right flank the next day, June 22.[17]

Alternate Scenario

Had he not relocated Hood, Johnston most likely would have taken one of two actions: ordering Hardee's Corps to shift southward and building a new defensive line to block Sherman's maneuvering around the Powder Springs Road, or ordering another command to position troops south of Hardee. Interestingly, in a June 2 letter to his wife, Mary, Hardee mentioned that he believed Johnston was relying more on Hood than on him. Johnston could have filled the vacated positions by further stretching his remaining troops. However, the benefit to Johnston and the Confederacy would have been that, not being present, Hood would not have engaged the Federals in what became the Battle of Kolb's Farm. Perhaps another action of a different form might have taken place.[18]

Hood Orders an Attack on the Newly Deployed Union Right Flank

Situation

Lieut. Gen. John B. Hood had risen through the ranks as an excellent combat commander. A native of the Commonwealth of Kentucky, Hood graduated forty-fifth of fifty-five from West Point in the class of 1847. After serving in California and Texas, he resigned from the US Army in 1861 to enter Confederate service. Advancing in spectacular fashion, he quickly rose from regimental to brigade to division command in Gen. Robert E. Lee's Army of Northern Virginia. Attaining success in several direct charges against the enemy, Hood advocated using such assaults to achieve victory. Wounded in the arm at Gettysburg on the second day of fighting, he quickly recovered. Hood was then ordered west under Lieut. Gen. James Longstreet, where he fought at the Battle of Chickamauga. On the final day of combat there, Hood participated in the assault on an unplanned opening in the Union line, losing a leg in the process. Recovering in Richmond, he became a companion of Davis, who soon promoted him to lieutenant general. Johnston requested that Hood command one of his corps in 1864.[19]

Per Johnston's orders on June 21 (see discussion of the previous critical decision), Hood and his corps evacuated their position on the Confederate right flank and marched behind (east of) Kennesaw Mountain through Marietta. The corps camped about two miles west of Marietta.[20]

On July 22 Hood and his command marched away from the environs of Marietta. They traveled west to rejoin Johnston's Kennesaw Mountain Line, extending it south from where Hardee's Corps had established strong entrenchments. Johnston had selected and ordered Hood, not Hardee, to protect the all-important Western and Atlantic Railroad by not allowing the Union forces positioned near the Powder Springs Road to advance farther east.[21]

By afternoon Hood reached the area just south of Lieut. Gen. William J. Hardee's corps, until then commanding Johnston's left flank. Hood deployed his three divisions, commanded by Maj. Gens. Thomas C. Hindman, Carter L. Stevenson, and Alexander P. Stewart, from north to south facing roughly west toward the enemy. Hood initially positioned Hindman just south of Cheatham Hill, with Stevenson south of Hindman and straddling the Powder Springs Road. Stewart arrived later in the day and was designated the reserve.[22]

Options

Once positioned as Johnston's new left flank, Hood had three options. Having extended the rebel line to the south, he could order his men to erect fortifications for defense. A second course of action, likely in conjunction with the first, would be to dispatch skirmishers to develop the position of the Union line facing Hood. Finally, Hood could advance his corps directly at the Union line as a reconnaissance in force to either defeat it or otherwise discover its exact location.[23]

Option 1

Hood's orders from his commander were to halt any progress of Union forces attempting to continue east toward the railroad near Marietta. Johnston did not specifically order Hood to advance or attack. At this time, the rebel commander apparently wanted to maintain his Kennesaw Mountain Line and await Sherman's next move. Therefore, Hood should establish and fortify his new position and stand by for further orders.[24]

Option 2

While beginning to fortify his new line south of Hardee's, Hood, like most commanders, would logically wish to determine the enemy's position. Sending out parties of skirmishers would provide feedback as to the strength and location of the Federals. Hood could dispatch these soldiers without significantly affecting the efforts at fortification, and still follow Johnston's orders.[25]

Option 3

Hood's third option was to advance some or all of his three divisions as a reconnaissance in force to ascertain the location and strength of the opposing Yankees. This option would seemingly exceed his orders.[26]

Decision

Hood quickly decided to conduct a reconnaissance in force and advance west-southwest toward the enemy.[27]

Results/Impact

Hood initially decided to advance. Members of the Fourteenth Kentucky and Twenty-Third New York had been ordered to maneuver toward the rebel line as skirmishers, and they contributed to this choice. When his advance units contacted these Federals, Hood apparently believed them to be assaulting his force, and he ordered an assault in turn. Hindman's Division advanced north of the Powder Springs Road, while Stevenson's Division moved even with Hindman to his left. Stewart's Division remained behind as the reserve.[28]

Reasonably concerned that the Yankees might discover his movement, Hood advanced largely blind against a foe of undetermined size. The terrain further hampered his efforts. Trees, dense undergrowth, and ravines provided continuous obstacles to the rebel advance. While initially an impediment, at least one ravine became a place of shelter for the men of Hindman's Division.[29]

As discussed in regard to an earlier critical decision, Sherman deployed Hooker's Twentieth Corps and Schofield's Twenty-Third Corps to extend his right flank with the possibility of advancing around Johnston's left flank. As was typical of the times, these troops immediately began to erect fortifications. Hooker's divisions commanded by Brig. Gens. Alpheus S. Williams and John W. Geary dug in north of the Powder Springs Road. Williams's right was touching that road, and Geary was positioned to Williams's left. Eight Union batteries located along this line were available to provide artillery support. The Federal position was located on high ground commanding an open field of fire to the east-northeast. With additional support on both flanks, the Yankees presented a very formidable force of some fourteen thousand soldiers compared to Hood's eleven thousand.[30]

Without any specific orders to do so, Hood committed his corps to fight

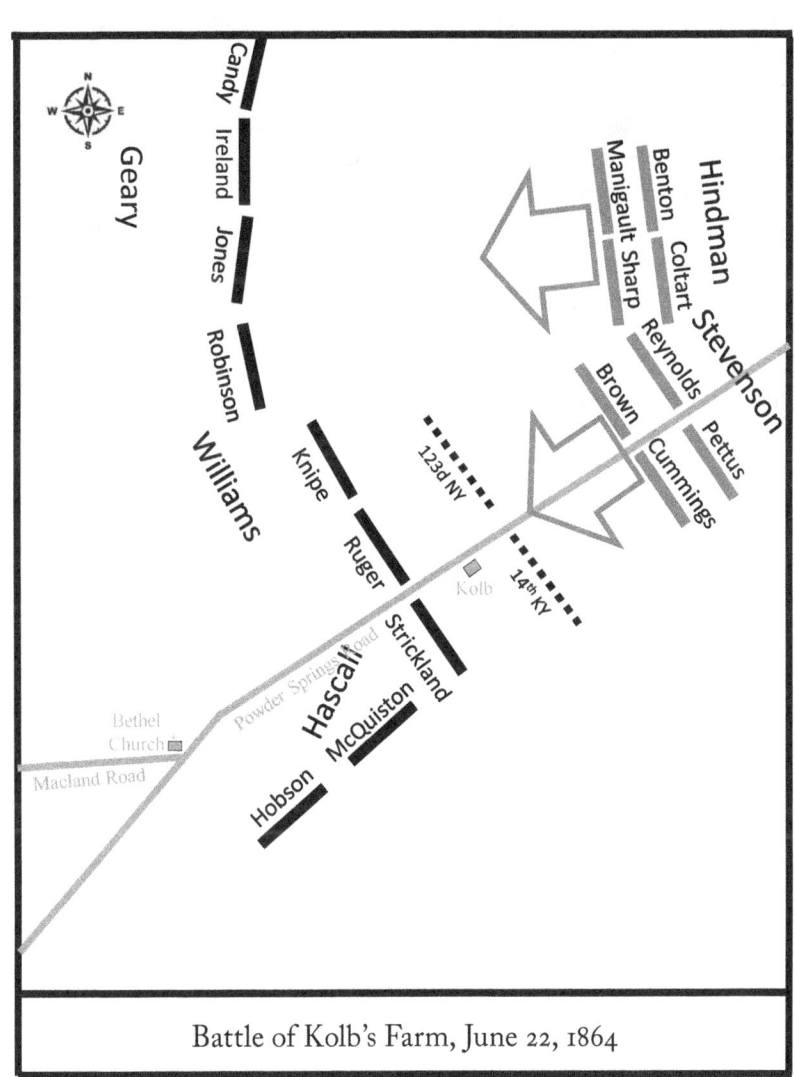

Battle of Kolb's Farm, June 22, 1864

the Federals, ordering the advance around 5:00 p.m. Warned by skirmishers, the Yankees waited. At close range the Union divisions and artillery opened fire on the rebels, seriously damaging Hood's Corps. Where possible, the Confederate troops retreated into some of the ravines they had passed through. However, shot and shell continued to rain down on them. Hood ordered Stewart's Division to advance on Hood's left, but it hardly engaged in combat before being recalled.[31]

This small battle ended quickly, with Hood withdrawing to an extension of the Confederate line south of Cheatham Hill. He suffered about 1,500 casualties, with Stevenson's Division alone losing 807 irreplaceable soldiers. Union casualties were listed as fewer than 250. Albert Castel characterized this action as more of a one-sided slaughter than a battle.[32]

Though Hood's force was defeated around Kolb's Farm, nonetheless his presence temporarily ended any additional flanking by the Union. He successfully followed Johnston's orders to protect the Confederate army's left flank. Sherman had stretched his line about as far as he could. Therefore, Sherman needed to reassess his situation and devise another tactic. This he did, resulting in the Battle of Kennesaw Mountain. Thus Hood's "affair" at Kolb's Farm was not in vain.[33]

While having perhaps no effect on the upcoming battle, an interesting aside is that Hooker claimed that his corps faced all three of Johnston's corps. Sherman, knowing that this was simply preposterous, met with Hooker the following day. The Union commander recalled the encounter as follows: "I told him [Hooker] that such a thing must not occur again; in other words I reproved him more gently than the occasion demanded, and from that time he began to sulk."[34]

Alternate Scenario

Had Hood simply obeyed his orders, extending and strengthening the Confederate left flank, and positioning his men in line south of Hardee's Corps, he would not have ordered the assault known as the Battle of Kolb's Farm. This would have continued to discourage Sherman from attempting to outflank Johnston. Just as importantly, the Confederacy would not have lost 1,000 to 1,500 irreplaceable soldiers, depending on the actual number of casualties incurred. Hood's decision was costly to the Confederacy.[35]

CHAPTER 3

THE BATTLE OF KENNESAW MOUNTAIN JUNE 27, 1864

Two critical decisions formed the actual Battle of Kennesaw Mountain. Maj. Gen. William T. Sherman made one, and his commanders were responsible for the other. While not a huge battle causing extensive casualties, this engagement was an important part of the Atlanta Campaign.

Sherman Orders an Assault on the Center of the Kennesaw Mountain Line

Situation

Sherman had grown tired of outflanking Gen. Joseph E. Johnston; he desired to confront him in battle, where he had the edge in manpower. As discussed in the previous chapter, Johnston had at least temporarily halted Sherman's latest attempt at flanking. The Confederate Kennesaw Mountain Line extended over seven miles, while the Union line stretched some ten or more miles. "Cump" Sherman now pondered whether the rebel line that extended almost as far as possible had any weaknesses, specifically in the center. He was well aware of the Confederate commander's penchant for keeping his flanks strong. Sherman thus began considering several options. He knew that he could not simply remain in his trenches, as this would allow Johnston to further shift troops as desired. Such freedom would reinforce the rebel commander's strategy of successful retreats to defensible positions, which was already being seriously criticized by the Confederate government. To the dismay of the Confederacy, Johnston had already retreated some seventy miles south, rather than attempting to hold back Sherman's army group.[1]

Options

Since Sherman found himself at least temporarily stymied in front of Johnston's Kennesaw Mountain Line, he debated four options for proceeding. He might examine the possibility of outflanking Johnston's right along the railroad. Although the Federals had already been rebuffed, retrying to outflank the rebel left might finally succeed. Sherman could also continue to hold Johnston in place by carefully advancing his trenches while maintaining artillery fire on the rebels. Finally, he could order a general assault by his combined armies (considered an army group today) at potentially vulnerable locations along the Confederate line.[2]

Option 1

As the rebel commander had shifted Lieut. Gen. John B. Hood's corps from his right flank to his left, the right might now remain exposed to an attempt to bypass it. Certainly, the right flank posed less of a threat than it had prior to Hood's relocation. Up until now, Sherman had continuously turned Johnston's left flank with success. Why not try the right flank? Apparently, elements of Maj. Gen. Joseph Wheeler's cavalry corps provided the only protection covering Johnston's right.[3]

The problem with this option was the Western and Atlantic Railroad, the Union army's (army group's) source of supply. Cump knew that he must maintain total control of this supply line; if he did otherwise, his armies could not maintain their positions this far into rebel territory. Moving on the Confederate right flank invited an immediate counterattack, and it might very well result in further rebel movement to destroy at least some of the railroad. Would Sherman be able to react quickly enough if the Confederate defenders assumed the offense?[4]

Option 2

Sherman had already tried to move around Johnston's left flank, but the relocation of Hood's Corps at least temporarily stymied that maneuver. Yet Hood stretched his line south from Lieut. Gen. William J. Hardee's corps. Could

Sherman outreach the Confederate left flank as he had previously done at Dalton, Resaca, and the Mud Creek Line? Hood, guarding the rebel left flank, had recently lost up to fifteen hundred soldiers of his command at the Battle of Kolb's Farm. While his line was already heavily fortified, he might not be able to extend it farther. Outnumbering Johnston, Sherman might take advantage of his superior numbers once again.[5]

The important drawback to further extension of his line was that Sherman must continue to control the railroad, as discussed above. If he stretched his line any farther, the Union commander would have to weaken his left, making it a more inviting target. This would give Confederates the opportunity to cut the railroad at least temporarily and deprive the Yankees of required supplies. This maneuver might force the abandonment of any Union advance, as the Federals would have to recapture and rebuild the railroad. Another consideration was the weather. It had continued to rain, rendering movement on the roads virtually impossible.[6]

Option 3

The Union commander could use a different tactic—continue to confront and hold Johnston along his Kennesaw Mountain Line. Sherman might carefully and safely advance his line of entrenchments and order continuous artillery fire on the rebel line, forcing enemy troops to hunker down. This should focus Confederate attention to safely maintain the already heavily fortified and reinforced line they had constructed and wear down the Confederate army.[7]

The downside to this option was that it could potentially allow Johnston to hold Sherman in place. More importantly, the Union high command would view any halt to the army's advance as unacceptable. This negative viewpoint was obviously not in Sherman's best interests.[8]

Option 4

Having tired of flanking, Sherman could order an assault on the Kennesaw Mountain Line when the rain stopped and the ground dried out. He had sufficient manpower to try to overrun and split the line in at least a few locations. Perhaps he could catch the rebels by surprise. If he did so, Sherman would prove that he was not afraid to use assaults as another weapon against the rebels, and he would demonstrate to his men that he meant to achieve success.[9]

The obvious problem with this option was the likelihood that the Union forces involved would suffer high numbers of casualties. By this time in the war, soldiers on both sides knew that it was virtually impossible to successfully assault fortifications. Even if the defenses were overrun, the cost in casualties was usually too high. While useless assaults were even more costly to the Confederacy in terms of loss of irreplaceable soldiers, the citizens of the North had also come to despise these pointless attacks. Also, Sherman did not have the temperament to send his men to their deaths in great numbers. This trait was found in Lieut. Gen. Ulysses S. Grant, who generally won his battles and campaigns.[10]

Looking back on Sherman's record so far in the Atlanta Campaign, as commander he had ordered assaults at Resaca, New Hope Church, and Pickett's Mill. The fighting at Resaca consisted more of probes back and forth by both sides rather than an all-out assault. The other attacks involved only a small portion of his force.[11]

Decision

After some consideration, Sherman focused his assault on potentially vulnerable locations of the Kennesaw Mountain Line.[12]

Results/Impact

On June 24 Sherman issued Special Field Orders Number 28 to his commanders outlining his plan of assault. He rationalized that with Johnston's line stretched to the limit, it would be weakest in the center, with the rebel focus on the flanks. Sherman ordered Maj. Gen. George H. Thomas to strike somewhere in the center of the Kennesaw Mountain Line and Maj. Gen. James B. McPherson to attack southwest of Kennesaw Mountain. The major generals would also simultaneously conduct diversionary movements. He also ordered Maj. Gen. John M. Schofield to attack at some point near the Powder Springs Road.[13]

The Union commander also mandated that these orders be kept secret. However, since both Thomas and McPherson had to move their divisions in preparation for the assaults, the men deduced that something was up. Not surprisingly, Thomas selected the salient at Cheatham Hill and the line just north of it as his point of attack. While certainly vulnerable, the final part of the advance toward this location was steeply uphill into a solidly fortified rebel position. Brig. Gen. John Newton's division of Maj. Gen. Oliver O. Howard's Fourth Corps and Brig. Gen. Jefferson C. Davis's division of Maj. Gen. John M. Palmer's Fourteenth Corps were chosen for the assault.[14]

Newton's division consisted of the brigades of Brig. Gens. Nathan Kimball, George D. Wagner, and Charles G. Harker, all of which would assault the Kennesaw Mountain Line. Kimball's brigade would advance toward Confederate Brig. Gen. Lucius Polk's brigade of Maj. Gen. Patrick R.

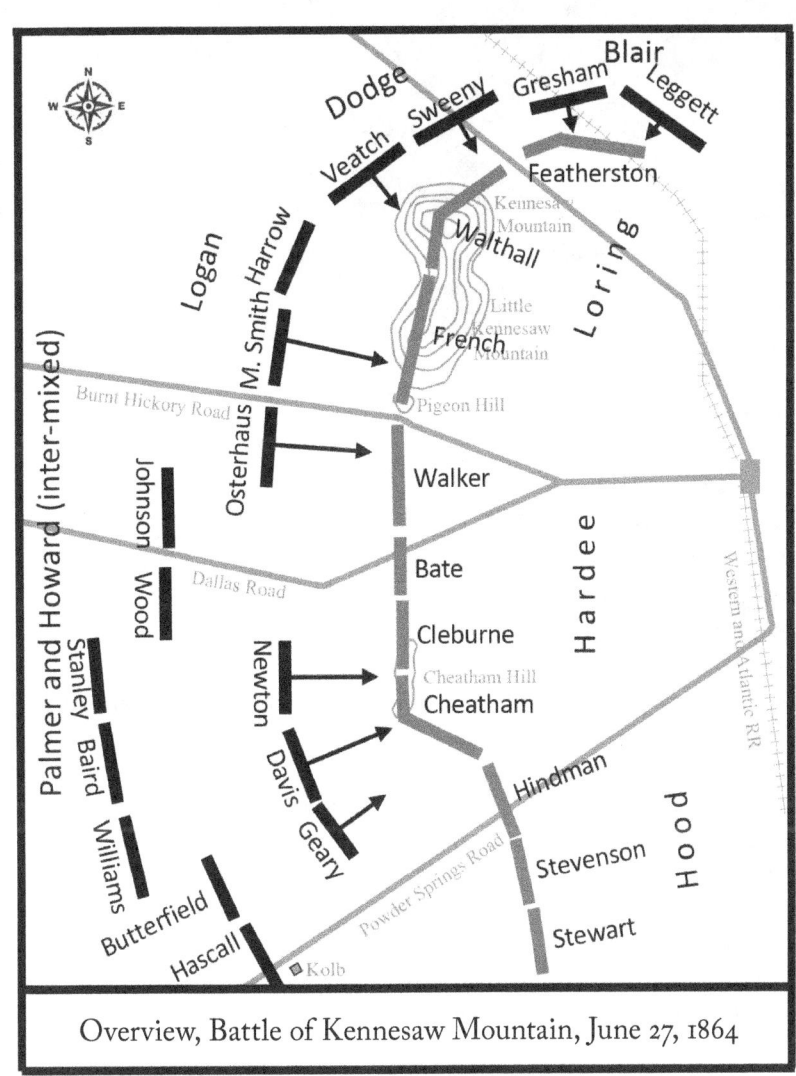

Overview, Battle of Kennesaw Mountain, June 27, 1864

Brig. Gen. Charles G. Harker, USA. *Photographic History of the Civil War*, Vol. 10, 139.

Cleburne's division. Cleburne's command was positioned immediately north of Brig. Gen. Alfred J. Vaughan's brigade, defending the northern part of Cheatham Hill. Wagner was to advance on Kimball's right, while Harker would strike just north of the Dead Angle itself. These three brigades provided around five thousand men to carry the assault.[15]

The brigades of Col. Daniel McCook and Col. John G. Mitchell of Davis's division would join the assault south of Harker. McCook would aim directly for the front of the salient at Cheatham Hill. Mitchell would be positioned on his right flank to strike Brig. Gen. George E. Maney's brigade, which was defending the nose and south part of the salient. Davis's third brigade, that of Brig. Gen. James D. Morgan, would follow behind McCook and Mitchell as the reserve. The two lead brigades totaled about four thousand troops.[16]

McPherson began to ready his command for the upcoming assault ordered by Sherman. After Davis's and Brig. Gen. Absalom Baird's divisions of the Fourth Corps shifted farther south, in preparation for their own assaults, McPherson moved Maj. Gen. John A. Logan's Fifteenth Corps from north of Kennesaw Mountain to west of Kennesaw Spur, the name of Pigeon Hill during the battle, and the focus of McPherson's assault. Logan commanded four divisions under Brig. Gens. Peter J. Osterhaus, Morgan L. Smith, John E. Smith, and William Harrow. Osterhaus's brigades, led by Brig. Gen. Charles R. Woods and Cols. James A. Williamson and Hugo Wangelin, would remain in reserve. Morgan L. Smith would launch his two brigades under the command of Brig. Gens. Giles A. Smith (his brother) and Joseph Lightburn. Giles A. Smith moved southeast just north of Burnt Hickory Road, and Lightburn attacking east next to him and just south of that road. John E. Smith's division was not involved, as it guarded the railroad around Cartersville. Harrow's division would contribute Brig. Gen. Charles C. Walcutt's brigade to the upcoming fray, advancing southeast on the left flank of Giles Smith. Logan supplied some 5,500 men in total for the assault. McPherson would also order diversionary assaults by units of his Sixteenth Corps north of Harrow and his Seventeenth Corps north and east of Kennesaw Mountain.[17]

On June 25 Sherman modified his orders slightly by canceling Schofield's assault. Instead, he had Schofield move Brig. Gen. Jacob D. Cox's division south across Olley's Creek. The Union commander hoped that once the rebels noticed this movement they might shift troops to Cox's new location, and away from the planned assault positions of McPherson and Thomas. Likewise, this repositioning might detract Johnston's attention.[18]

All these preparations set the stage for the assault ordered on June 27. Yet another critical decision contributed significantly to the outcome of the Battle of Kennesaw Mountain.

Union Commanders Assault Using Columns of Brigades

Situation

Thomas, Howard, and Newton were all kept busy making preparations for the upcoming offensive on June 27. In addition to selecting the intended target, they determined which commands would participate in the attack and moved them into position to commence it on time. Although Sherman's orders were to keep the planned assault secret, the troops could sense something was up.[19]

Options

Having designated the target of the assault, Thomas, Howard, and Newton had to decide how to organize the attacking brigades to carry out their orders most successfully. The two options were to advance their brigades in the standard linear formation or to maneuver in a column of brigades.[20]

Option 1

Per the military texts of the time and what was considered normal procedure, units would advance against the enemy in a linear formation. This arrangement would provide the greatest firepower once the attacking units moved within range to fire. Typically, a linear formation would have the regiments and brigades in two lines, allowing one line to fire while the other reloaded. The theory was that the resulting continuous fire would force defending enemy combatants to literally keep their heads down to avoid being hit. If effective, a linear formation would allow the attacking force to proceed while taking fewer casualties.[21]

The downside of this or any other offensive formation was that a well-fortified defense, especially one protected with head logs, could open fire on the assaulting units as soon as they advanced within range. Defending fire remained sustained with very limited casualties until the enemy units either overran the defensive fortifications or were forced to retreat. Adding artillery fire, especially canister and double-shotted canister, would give the defense an even more decisive advantage, especially if its artillery was protected from enemy fire.[22]

Option 2

A reputed better method of assault was one ordered in a column of brigades. This required regiments to line up in five rows of two companies each, with one regiment after the other. This formation provided the narrowest and deepest one possible, and it presumed the best opportunity to penetrate the enemy's line. A force attacking "on the double," or twice as fast as the normal marching cadence, might catch the enemy off guard.[23]

The drawback to this style of attack was that if and when the leading regiments reached a stopping point, those behind would either continue on, trampling the lead soldiers, or spread out, losing effectiveness. Also, those in the rear ranks would be unable to fire without causing casualties among their own men. While this method appeared to be more successful, it was usually ineffective, if not downright dangerous to its participants. The soldiers involved dreaded the concept.[24]

Decision

Newton convinced Howard and Palmer to use the column of brigades for the assault, and Davis also ordered the same formation.[25]

Results/Impact

In theory, using this formation would result in a better chance of success. In this situation, however, it only made things worse for the attacking soldiers and proved detrimental to the outcome of the combined assaults. Both Kimball and Harker protested the designated arrangement, but Newton

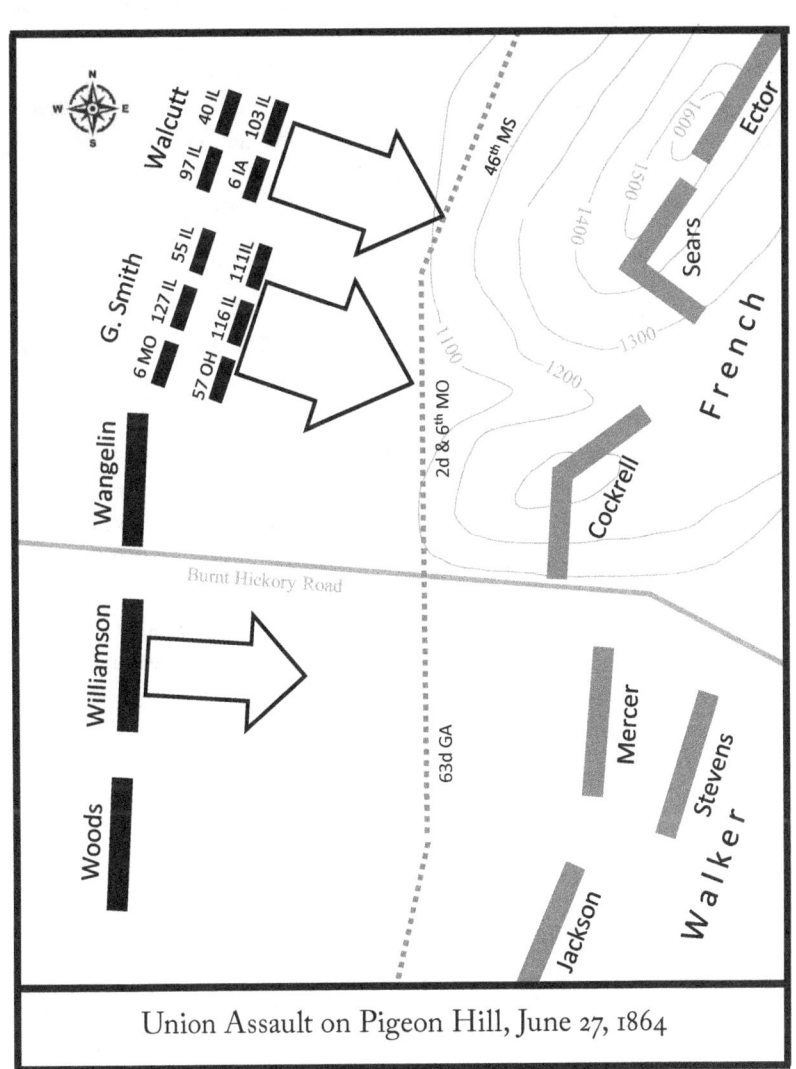

Union Assault on Pigeon Hill, June 27, 1864

overruled them, stating that the decision had already been made by higher headquarters.[26]

Before we review the effects of this critical decision on the battle, we will briefly describe the efforts of Logan's Fifteenth Corps and its assault on Kennesaw Spur (Pigeon Hill). Logan's men advanced in standard battle formation, not using the column of brigades. Upon receiving the order to advance, Lightburn's brigade moved east just south of the Burnt Hickory Road. Heavy Confederate resistance stymied the unit's advance. However, Lightburn's left flank regiment, the Fifty-Fourth Ohio, changed front and maneuvered northeast toward rebel brigadier general Francis M. Cockrell's brigade defending the spur. Maj. Gen. Samuel G. French, Cockrell's division commander, dispatched reinforcements that helped Cockrell defend his position.[27]

North of Lightburn, the brigades of Brig. Gen. Giles A. Smith and Brig. Gen. Charles C. Walcutt assaulted the Kennesaw Spur. While quickly overrunning the rebel pickets, both brigades soon ground to a halt as the Confederate defenders poured destructive fire on them. In many cases the soldiers of these Union regiments were not even able to retreat until darkness provided adequate protection.[28]

The rest of Logan's Fifteenth Corps and McPherson's two other corps, the Sixteenth and Seventeenth, conducted demonstrations along McPherson's entire line northwest and north of Kennesaw Mountain. While McPherson's soldiers generally drove back the Confederate skirmishers and maintained the appearance of a major engagement, no substantial gains were expected or made. The other truth that emerged from McPherson's engagements was that his men discovered no weak points in the Southern line. The northern portion of Johnston's Kennesaw Mountain Line stood firm.[29]

The final lineup occurred west of Cheatham Hill. The brigades selected for the assault against that location lined up in a column of brigades, and their targets remained the same. Brig. Gen. Charles G. Harker's brigade would aim for the tip, or nose, of the salient on Cheatham Hill. To his immediate left were the brigades of Brig. Gens. George D. Wagner and Nathan Kimball; these were to strike Maj. Gen. Patrick Cleburne's division, which was next in line to Brig. Gen. Alfred J. Vaughan's brigade defending the northern half of the salient. Likewise, Col. Daniel McCook's brigade started toward the front of the hill just south of Harker. Brig. Gen. John G. Mitchell's advanced immediately south, en route to strike Brig. Gen. George E. Maney's brigade defending the south half of the salient.[30]

After an artillery barrage from 8:00 to 8:15 a.m., all five brigades advanced from just east of Sherman's headquarters, marching down across a branch of

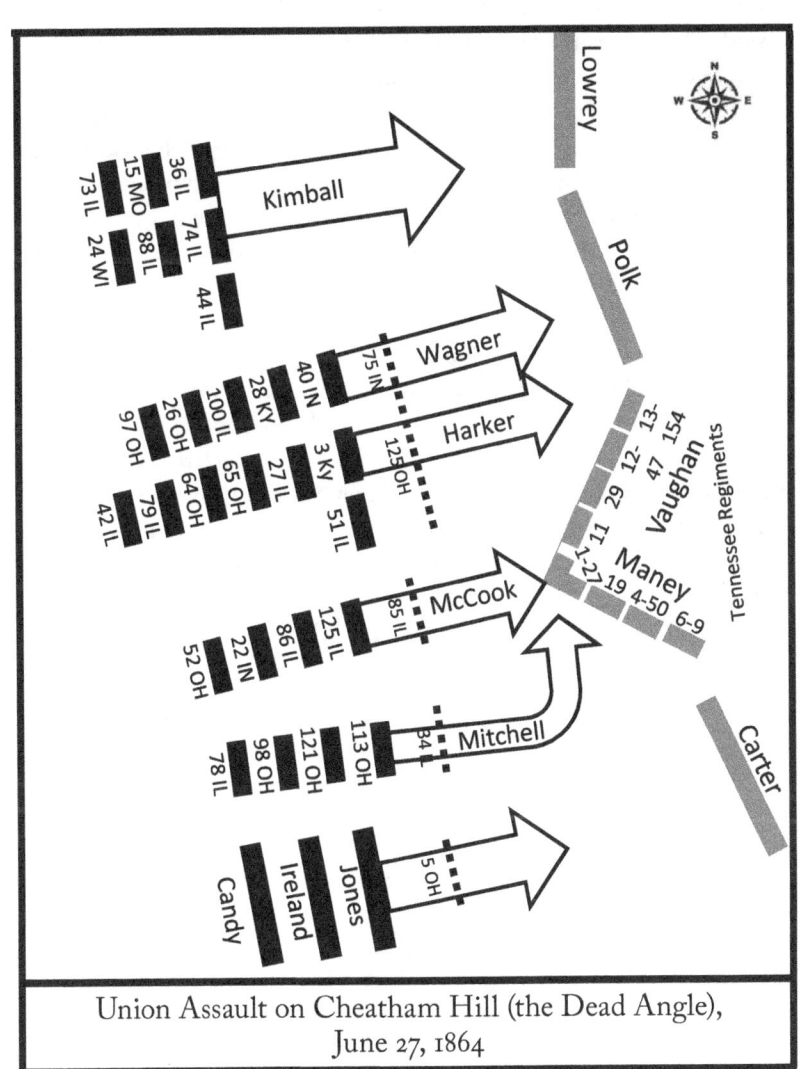

Union Assault on Cheatham Hill (the Dead Angle), June 27, 1864

John Ward Creek, then up the steep slope leading to the Confederate defenses on Cheatham Hill. This was a journey of some seven to eight hundred yards, depending on the specific unit. In 1902 J. B. Work, a member of the Col. Dan McCook Brigade Association, measured the distance McCook's brigade traveled to the rebel fortifications on Cheatham Hill as exactly 1,743 feet, or 581 yards. As soon as the Federal troops moved within range of the Confederates, they opened a deadly fire, including the artillery hidden by Maj. Gen. Benjamin F. Cheatham, as discussed concerning an earlier critical decision.[31]

The brigades of Kimball and Wagner assaulted Cleburne's lines in column formation, but, as many of their men had predicted, they quickly fell apart. Evidence indicates that Harker apparently did not conform to the formation as ordered. Additionally, he ordered his men to load their weapons but not cap them to prevent them from stopping to shoot. Overwhelming rebel fire generally stopped the Federals before they could reach the Confederate line, forcing them to seek shelter behind the abatis and any tree or ground providing protection. During the assault, Harker was mortally wounded.[32]

An interesting interlude occurred during this portion of the Union assault. Because of the heavy fire, the grass, leaves, and underbrush caught on fire, endangering the many wounded Union soldiers lying on the ground. Confederate Lieut. Col. William H. Martin, commanding the First and Fifteenth Arkansas, bravely leaped up on top of his breastworks with a white flag of truce and declared that the Yankees must quickly remove these wounded. This was done with the help of some of the rebels. During this truce some

Col. Daniel McCook Jr., USA.
Photographic History of the Civil War,
Vol. 10, 139.

Yankees apparently picked up abandoned weapons, while Confederates might have closely observed the Union fortifications. Then the killing resumed.[33]

The brigades of McCook and Mitchell advanced at the same time, making straight for the salient at the Dead Angle and the area just south of it. As ordered, they advanced in a column of regiments. Prior to McCook's advance, in an effort to motivate his men, he might have quoted from the poet Horatius (This event is described in discussion of Stop 5B on the driving tour provided in appendix I.) McCook insisted on riding his horse, which made him an easy target. As the men of both of these brigades advanced in range of the Confederates commanded by Vaughan and Maney, the rebels opened up a withering fire, mowing down the Yankees by the score. Protected behind their breastworks complete with head logs, the rebels could not fail to strike a Union soldier with virtually every shot, and the slaughter continued. A few Yankees made it to the Confederate fortifications, including Colonel McCook, but these men were quickly killed, wounded, or captured by being pulled into the rebel trenches. McCook was mortally wounded.[34]

Mitchell's brigade advanced into the same barrage of fire and was unable to carry the rebel works. His men, like those in the other brigades, were caught in a death trap. They couldn't go forward, and retreating meant good odds of being shot in the back. However, in an interesting turn of events, as we will see in regard to the next critical decision, another option was available.[35]

General Vaughan had been told by his commanders that he must hold his position at the Dead Angle on Cheatham Hill if it required the loss of

Brig. Gen. Alfred J. Vaughan Jr., CSA. *Photographic History of the Civil War*, Vol. 10, 299.

Brig. Gen. George Maney, CSA. *Photographic History of the Civil War,* Vol. 10, 295.

every soldier. Vaughan himself later wrote of the Union assault, "In column seven lines deep, with not a cap on the guns of the first two lines, he [Harker] attempted to storm our position. Never did men march into the very jaws of death with a firmer tread and with more determination than did the Federals to this attack. But they met intrenched infantry, and the concentrated fire of musketry, canister, grapeshot and shell mowed them down at every step. Yet they still struggled forward, but every Confederate stood at his post, and in a short time it was more than mortals could stand and they broke and fled, leaving eight hundred of their dead."[36]

Pvt. Sam Watkins of the First Tennessee in Maney's Brigade gave a very vivid description of the fighting: "When the Yankees fell back, and the firing ceased, I never saw so many broken down and exhausted men in my life. I was as sick as a horse, and as wet with blood and sweat as I could be, and many of our men were vomiting with excessive fatigue, over exhaustion, and sunstroke; our tongues were parched and cracked for water, and our faces blackened with powder and smoke, and our dead and wounded were piled indiscriminately in the trenches. There was not a single man in the company who was not wounded, or had holes shot through his hat and clothing."[37]

By around 10:45 a.m. the Union high command realized that the assaults had failed. The aggregate number of Federal casualties approximated three thousand. One thousand dead Yankees lay directly in front of the Dead

Angle, contributing to its label. The 125th Illinois, the leading regiment of McCook's brigade, suffered a 60 percent casualty rate during the assault. This is one major reason why the Illinois Monument is located at the Dead Angle on Cheatham Hill. The Fifty-Second Ohio of the same brigade lost 43 percent of its men. Overall, McCook's brigade lost 38 percent of its soldiers. In Mitchell's brigade the 130th and 121st Ohio regiments, which led the assault, lost almost half of their men to casualties. The rebels lost around seven hundred troops.[38]

With one important exception to be discussed next, the battle was over, and Sherman had lost. He asked Thomas whether to order soldiers to prepare for additional assaults. Thomas famously replied, "We have already lost heavily to-day without gaining any material advantage; one or two more such assaults would use up this army." This defeat reinforced his strategy to continue to outflank Johnston when possible, as the rebel commander seemed unlikely to ever attack Sherman. Yet the Union assault was not a total failure.[39]

As briefly noted above, as the Union assault fell apart, those soldiers still capable of movement had several choices for responding. If they hugged the ground or found a tree or other barrier from rebel rifle fire, they might survive until nightfall would allow them to sneak back to their lines. Turning around and retreating would likely get them shot in the back. However, the soldiers in McCook's and Mitchell's brigades found another way to survive.[40]

As discussed concerning a previous critical decision, the Confederate line defending the Dead Angle on Cheatham Hill followed the topographical crest, not the military crest. Therefore, the rebels defending that position discovered a small area in front where their fire could not reach any Yankees. As Federal soldiers began to retreat, they quickly discovered and took advantage of this location, which saved them from being shot in the back as they withdrew. This limited natural area of protection was only some thirty to fifty yards from the Confederate line. Though the site was initially filled with few soldiers, more and more men quickly joined them.[41]

After the horrible end to the Union assault, all that the soldiers who were lightly wounded or unwounded wanted was to escape back to their original lines. As noted, the chances of being shot in the back were so high that most did not risk it. Finding and hiding behind any form of protection was foremost on their minds. Discovering the small location in front of the Dead Angle was the temporary shelter needed. The men attempted to hide here and even return some of the rebel fire, surviving until the cover of night allowed them to flee back to their lines. They simply had to keep themselves away from the deadly fire by building minimal fortifications.[42]

Another possibility was taking advantage of this very forward position and establishing a well-fortified line from which to fire on the Confederates. This was a very dangerous location, and the Federals would have to take care to continuously man it. It provided a small amount of success during the otherwise disastrous morning's assaults.[43]

It quickly dawned on the Federal soldiers desperately seeking shelter along this small, protected area that if they could eventually fortify their new line, they would be able to return the rebel fire and potentially launch another assault. Not only did they continue to establish whatever fortifications they could, but they also sought help. Union troops manned the new line in the coming days.[44]

The Federals rotated in and out of this line at night and resupplied their comrades-in-arms. They also fired anytime they spotted a Confederate soldier peering over the rebel breastworks. It was extremely dangerous for any combatant to expose any part of his body to enemy fire, so both sides were on constant watch twenty-four hours a day. The rebels used fireballs at night to provide enough light to guard against a surprise attack.[45]

The Yankees quickly devised a better scheme to solve their predicament. They began to mine under the Dead Angle with the objective of blowing up a portion of it, thereby opening the way to penetrate the Confederate line. It

Illinois Monument and tunnel entrance, Kennesaw Mountain National Battlefield Park. Courtesy of Bill Gurry.

was only about one hundred feet from the Federal position to the Dead Angle. The rebels manning the Dead Angle's fortifications became aware of the potential mining efforts. However, the Kennesaw Line was abandoned before the work was completed.[46]

Another interesting aspect of the fighting here in the days after the main assault involved mirrors. Union soldiers in their fortifications used small mirrors to help them fire on the rebels while remaining in relative safety. Federals could remain protected while using this new tool to accurately aim their guns at the enemy. Because of this enhanced fire, the head logs that had afforded Confederate defenders a huge level of protection were shot to pieces after June 27.[47]

For the remainder of June and the first two days of July, both armies remained locked in position. By maintaining this line while preparing to blow up part of the Dead Angle, Union soldiers placed additional pressure on Johnston to abandon the position. The deadly fire continued day and night at the Dead Angle. However, Sherman continued to scheme.[48]

Alternate Scenario

Many wonder why Sherman ordered what appeared to be virtually hopeless assaults on the very well-fortified Kennesaw Mountain Line. As previously discussed, by this time in the Civil War Federals and Confederates erected strong fortifications anytime they halted for any length of time. Troops generally considered it impossible to successfully assault them. What if Sherman simply held off ordering his assault and perhaps inched his lines forward, keeping Johnston's army within its defenses? This would have saved some three thousand of the Yankee commander's men from becoming casualties.[49]

CHAPTER 4

AFTER THE BATTLE OF KENNESAW MOUNTAIN JUNE 28–JULY 3, 1864

After his unsuccessful assaults on Gen. Joseph E. Johnston's Kennesaw Mountain Line, Maj. Gen. William T. Sherman wasted little time in making a final critical decision relative to it. The weather finally began to cooperate.

Sherman Outflanks Johnston to Advance toward the Chattahoochee River

Situation

Like most graduates of West Point, Sherman preferred to win by maneuver rather than direct attack. The failed assault on June 27 reinforced his methodology of outflanking or using turning movements to force Johnston's Army of Tennessee to continue to retreat. After weeks of constant rain, the skies finally cleared, and the roads began to dry. This facilitated the Union commander's ability to again maneuver his army group as he desired. However, he needed to accumulate additional supplies before he could begin any movements.[1]

Another consideration Sherman constantly contended with was keeping Johnston too busy to send troops to Gen. Robert E. Lee in Virginia. (This concern was based on Johnston continuously retreating rather than confronting

Sherman. The latter eventuality was highly unlikely.) Coincidentally, on June 28 Sherman received a telegram from chief of staff Maj. Gen. Henry W. Halleck on behalf of general-in-chief Lieut. Gen. Ulysses S. Grant that relieved him of that duty. Grant now believed that Lee could not order additional troops to Virginia because he was unable to feed them. This meant that Sherman now was free to maneuver as he desired. What orders would he next give to his armies?[2]

Options

The group commander evaluated two options. He might try outflanking Johnston on his right flank, or he could make another attempt at bypassing the rebel commander on his left flank. These turning movements should force Johnston to continue retreating, as he refused to attack the Union army group directly.[3]

Option 1

Maneuvering past Johnston's right flank would allow Sherman to move along the railroad. Unfortunately, it would also leave this supply line vulnerable to being recaptured by Johnston.[4]

Option 2

With his right flank already maneuvering past Johnston's left, Sherman could position his armies to outflank the rebel commander's left once again. Sherman could potentially march straight to the Chattahoochee River; he was actually closer to it than Johnston was.[5]

Decision

With the weather generally cooperating, Sherman quickly decided to flank Johnston's left, and he ordered Maj. Gen. James B. McPherson's Army of the Tennessee to further extend his right. Sherman's new goal was Fulton, now Smyrna, on the railroad south of Marietta.[6]

Results/Impact

While accumulating supplies to allow the Federals to leave the railroad temporarily, Sherman continued to shift his men south in preparation for an advance toward Fulton. From the top of Kennesaw Mountain, the Confederates observed Federal movements and predicted that the Union commander was preparing another turning movement.[7]

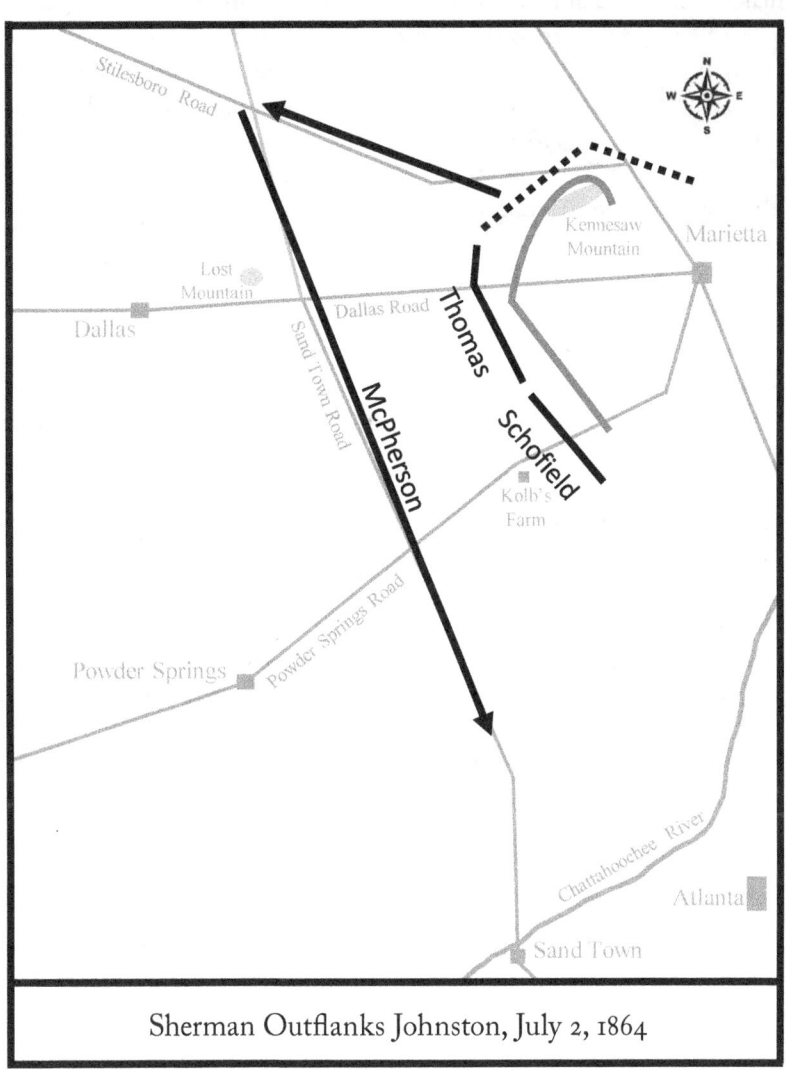

Sherman Outflanks Johnston, July 2, 1864

Maj. Gen. John Schofield offered Sherman an interesting possibility to consider: What if Johnston decided to remain fortified around Kennesaw Mountain, protected by new entrenchments in his vulnerable rear, and fortified with several weeks' worth of accumulated supplies? The Union commander replied, "I am not bound to attack him in his position after getting below him, but may cross the Chattahoochee and destroy all his railroads before he can prevent it, which will be a desperate game for both of us." In reality, the rebel commander continued to request additional cavalry to cut the railroad in Sherman's rear.[8]

As previously noted, deadly sharpshooting continued around Cheatham Hill both day and night. The Yankees persisted in fortifying their meager works. Apparently some units rotated in and out, while others presumably hung on for days on end. Due to the putridness of the hundreds of Union corpses lying in the extremely hot sun, on June 29 a truce was declared in order to bury these bodies. As the work of burying continued, men from both sides chatted and examined one another. Once the truce was over, they immediately began exchanging fire. Work continued on the mine, eventually coming within feet of the rebel works.[9]

General Johnston concluded that the Yankee commander was in the process of outflanking him once again. Sen. Benjamin Hill visited Johnston on July 1 and was astonished to learn that the Confederate commander had no real plan to defeat Sherman! Johnston ordered a withdrawal to what would be labeled the Smyrna Line on the night of July 2. He issued orders for a clandestine movement, which proved entirely successful. The Federal soldiers were pleasantly surprised to discover the rebels gone from their Kennesaw Mountain Line.[10]

Once Sherman discovered the rebel pullout, he concluded that Johnston would retreat across the Chattahoochee River, as no commander would have his back to a river (although the Confederate commander had previously done so at Resaca with the Oostanaula River behind his lines). The Union commander ordered his armies to advance toward Fulton. He had successfully turned Johnston out of his Kennesaw Mountain Line, forcing a retreat. Although Sherman had lost the battle, he continued to advance toward Atlanta and would eventually capture it, winning the Atlanta Campaign.[11]

CHAPTER 5

AFTERMATH AND CONCLUSIONS

Not surprisingly, all of the critical decisions of the Battle of Kennesaw Mountain were tactical in nature, since this engagement took place in the midst of a major campaign. The Federal and Confederate governments had already appointed their senior commanders to guide the course of the Atlanta Campaign. Logistics and supply lines established by the two sides had been continuously in use. Some eight turning movements by Maj. Gen. William T. Sherman and his army group brought the armies to the Kennesaw Mountain Line.[1]

The Union commander was (and is) often criticized for squandering some three thousand of his men. On reflection, he largely agreed. On June 29 Sherman wrote his wife, Ellen,

> It is enough to make the whole world start at the awful amount of death and Destruction that now stalks abroad.... I begin to regard the death and mangling of a couple of thousand men as a small affair, a kind of morning dash—and it may be well that we become hardened.... The worst of the war is not yet begun.

However, Sherman's decision to assault appeared logical at the time. In terms of the significance of his casualties, he began the campaign with 110,123 men and 254 guns. Johnston then had 54,500 present for duty and 144 guns. Federal losses up to July 17, a period including brief fighting on the Smyrna and

Chattahoochee River Lines after the Battle of Kennesaw Mountain, were around 17,200, as compared with the Confederates' 10,760. Considering that Sherman was down to around 93,923 men, this provides a casualty percentage of 3.2 percent. This loss in terms of the big picture is not overly significant, especially when compared with the horrific losses suffered by Lieut. Gen. Ulysses S. Grant and Maj. Gen. George G. Meade during the Overland Campaign, including the Battles of the Wilderness and Spotsylvania. In four weeks, those officers' casualties totaled some 44,000 men.[2]

Johnston, of course, appreciated the outcome, as the Yankees finally assaulted him while he was well entrenched and prepared, seemingly his plan for the campaign. Estimates are that the rebel commander suffered only about seven hundred casualties on July 27. His methodology was vindicated by no less a personage than President Davis after the Battles of Peachtree Creek, Atlanta, and Ezra Church, as described below, where new army commander Gen. John B. Hood collectively lost some eleven thousand men. As Davis told Hood, "The loss consequent upon attacking him [Sherman] in his intrenchments requires you to avoid that if practicable." But Johnston had to guess that Sherman would simply continue using turning movements as he placed more and more of northwestern Georgia under Union control.[3]

Sherman waited until the weather allowed the roads to dry out and kept practicing his turning movements. At little additional cost he was able to turn Gen. Joseph E. Johnston out of his Kennesaw Mountain Line and maintain the Federal advance toward Atlanta. Many have argued that Sherman erred in attacking at Kennesaw Mountain, and twenty-twenty hindsight indicates that he did. Nonetheless, he continued the campaign to what became a successful conclusion for the Union.[4]

Sherman took advantage of the now-sunny weather to turn Johnston's left flank as described in the previous chapter. The Federal commander maneuvered his armies toward the railroad, expecting Johnston to retreat across the Chattahoochee River, as no commander would likely entrench with his back to a river. Johnston quickly withdrew, but only to a new defensive line labeled the Smyrna Line, situated a few miles north of the river. This new formation ran from east of the railroad near the Smyrna Campground southwest to Ruff's Mill. On July 4 this caught Sherman by surprise, and he ordered a reconnaissance in force against the Smyrna Line as his armies made several attempts to confirm the Confederate position.[5]

After temporarily holding the Yankees at bay, on the night of July 4, the Army of Tennessee retreated. However, it entrenched once again north of the Chattahoochee into a series of fortifications called Shoupades. New to both armies, these defenses were named for their designer, chief engineer Brig.

Gen. Francis A. Shoup. The unique design dubbed the Chattahoochee River Line generally did not impress the rebel defenders. Nonetheless, this line presented Sherman with another hurdle to overcome. Realizing its defensive strength, the Union commander tricked Johnston.[6]

During the entire campaign so far Sherman had always turned Johnston's left flank. This time, however, he decided to turn the Army of Tennessee's right flank. The Union commander ordered Maj. Gen. John Schofield's army to advance to Roswell and cross the Chattahoochee. On July 8 Schofield's divisions managed to cross, some at the city and others using an old fish dam. Once the Federals were established south of the river, Johnston had no choice but to retreat across the river as well, which he did on the night of July 9–10. This action caused a major turn of events.[7]

Everyone from President Jefferson Davis on down feared that Johnston's continuing retreats would provide a dire outcome for Atlanta, as well as for the Confederate Army of Tennessee. Davis demanded that Johnston inform him as to how he planned to halt Sherman's advance. The rebel commander's responses were vague and alarming—for example, he advocated abandoning the Confederate prisoner-of-war camp at Andersonville. After much consideration, on the evening of July 17, Davis replaced Johnston with John B. Hood, whom he temporarily elevated to the rank of general. Known as an aggressive commander, Hood realized he was expected to confront the Union armies. He wasted no time in doing so.[8]

Once the Union armies crossed the Chattahoochee, Sherman ordered Maj. Gen. James B. McPherson to have his Army of the Tennessee completely destroy a portion of the Georgia Railroad to hinder the shifting of rebel troops to Atlanta. McPherson marched east of Decatur and tore up many miles of track. Schofield's Army of the Ohio advanced toward Atlanta from northwest of McPherson, while Maj. Gen. George H. Thomas's Army of the Cumberland maneuvered from the river toward Buckhead, advancing more directly toward Atlanta.[9]

For once, the three Union armies were separated. This circumstance provided the new Confederate commander the opportunity to attack one Federal army with a better likelihood of success, especially while not entrenched. Hood ordered an assault on Thomas's army, hoping to catch it unsupported while crossing Peachtree Creek, which flowed into the Chattahoochee north of Atlanta. However, due to realignment required to protect the city, by the time Hood's troops were ready to commence the assault on July 20, Thomas's soldiers had crossed Peachtree Creek and were now less vulnerable. The resulting Battle of Peachtree Creek failed to produce a Confederate victory at the cost of several thousand rebel casualties. Hood would have to try another tactic.[10]

Although known as an offensive-minded general, Hood was wise enough to at least attempt to attack components of the various Union armies maneuvering in the open rather than to order direct assaults on entrenched Yankees. He directed Wheeler's Cavalry to attempt to capture the large Union wagon train at Decatur. When Sherman ordered Brig. Gen. Kenner Garrard's division of cavalry to wreck railroads south and east of Atlanta, this exposed McPherson's left flank, as no cavalry was present to provide reconnaissance. The new rebel commander contemplated another attempt at victory by ordering a night flanking march to catch McPherson's army while it was vulnerable as it marched from Decatur to Atlanta. Hood ordered Lieut. Gen. William J. Hardee's corps to begin a lengthy advance of some fifteen miles toward Decatur, beginning on the evening of July 21. Hardee's men were tired from their fighting at the Battle of Peachtree Creek, and by morning they had not gained their objective of attacking McPherson's army in its rear while marching to Atlanta. The decision was made to stop where they were and assault McPherson's divisions from the south and west, just outside Atlanta. It was afternoon before the rebels were ready to assault.[11]

Hardee's Corps finally attacked, but McPherson, concerned over this exact possibility, had ordered a division to guard against such an assault. The Federals were therefore somewhat prepared to resist. After a series of assaults on and around Bald, or Leggett's, Hill, east of today's downtown Atlanta, Hood ordered Maj. Gen. Benjamin F. Cheatham's corps (Hood's old corps) to enter the fray by advancing from its position guarding the eastern side of the city. After breaking through the Fifteenth Corps Union line facing west in a few locations, especially through the railroad cut east of the city, Maj. Gen. John A. "Blackjack" Logan rallied his corps and regained its hold on the ground just east of the city. What started as a grand scheme by Hood failed because not enough time was allowed for his men to get into the proper position. McPherson's typical caution paid off this time, but it unfortunately cost him his life when he mistakenly rode into a rebel line. This fight, named the Battle of Atlanta, cost Hood more thousands of irreplaceable casualties.[12]

After these two battles, Hood retreated into the fortifications protecting Atlanta. Sherman realized that he could not realistically attack these defenses. He continued to maneuver to cut the remaining two railroads supplying the rebel city with foodstuffs and ammunition. Hood dispatched new corps commander Lieut. Stephen D. Lee, who had replaced Cheatham, to march west and protect the Lick Skillet Road from Sherman. Orders from Shoup, now Hood's chief of staff, were as follows: "General Hood directs that you hold the enemy in check. The object is to prevent him from gaining the Lick Skillet Road." However, the Union commander had already sent Maj. Gen. Oliver O.

Howard, who had replaced the deceased McPherson, west with his Army of the Tennessee to prepare to sever the last railroads. Howard reached the road first and instinctively fortified his position near Ezra Church. Lee, unwisely on his own, decided to attack upon arrival. The result was a Confederate disaster, with the loss of some three thousand irreplaceable rebels. Famously, a Yankee picket yelled at his Confederate enemy after the Battle of Ezra Church, inquiring, "Well Johnny, how many of you are left?" The rebel replied, "Oh, about enough for another killing."[13]

Sherman continued to stretch his line southwest of Atlanta, but Hood did likewise. Finally, the Union commander decided to advance to bypass the rebels. He sent the Twentieth Corps to protect his supply line, the Western and Atlantic Railroad. With his six other corps, he moved west and then south, then struck the Atlanta and West Point Railroad at Fairburn. On August 29, his men destroyed miles of that railroad. Then they marched east to sever the only remaining railroad servicing the city, the Macon and Western.[14]

Hood ordered Hardee to move his corps, temporarily commanded by Maj. Gen. Patrick R. Cleburne, and Lee's Corps to Jonesboro to guard the remaining tracks. On the thirtieth, Hardee unsuccessfully attacked Howard's corps, only one of six Union corps present just west of Jonesboro. Hood, fearing this was only a feint, ordered Lee's Corps back to Atlanta. With only one corps available, Hardee then had to attempt to hold back the six Union corps. On the afternoon of September 1, Hardee was barely able to repulse assaults by the Fourteenth and Fifteenth Corps, but he quickly retired south six miles to Lovejoy's Station. The two-day Battle of Jonesboro failed to prevent the Yankees from severing the last railroad serving Atlanta, forcing Hood to abandon the city that evening. The mayor surrendered it the next day. Sherman sent chief of staff Henry Halleck a fateful message: "Atlanta is ours and fairly won." The capture of Atlanta, while not the original goal of the campaign, provided the political capital for Lincoln's reelection and continuation of the war to eventual Union success.[15]

Sherman's armies retired to Atlanta for much-needed rest, recuperation, and refitting. Hood regrouped his army and moved north, cutting the Western and Atlantic Railroad in several places, but he failed to do so at Allatoona Pass during an intense small battle there on October 5. However, the Union commander realized that it was a tough proposition to maintain this lengthy supply line, and that he was unlikely to catch Hood's army. Sherman thus devised a solution to the problem. Finally convincing general-in-chief Ulysses S. Grant, he reorganized his command, sending Maj. Gen. George H. Thomas with the Fourth and Twenty-Third Corps to Nashville to contain

Hood should he advance there. With the Fourteenth, Fifteenth, Seventeenth, and Twentieth Corps (the Sixteenth Corps was broken up to augment the others), split into two wings, on November 16 Sherman, after burning a significant portion of Atlanta, including anything of military value, began his March to the Sea.[16]

Hood then decided to advance into Tennessee, capture Nashville, and perhaps maneuver to the Ohio River. The rebel commander gathered supplies, obtained pontoons to cross the Tennessee River, and moved to Columbia, pursuing Schofield's army. He outflanked Schofield but failed to confront him at Spring Hill. Possibly annoyed by this failure, when he discovered the Union corps temporarily entrenched at Franklin while rebuilding a bridge to cross the Harpeth River, Hood ordered an all-out assault. With only two of his three corps present and no artillery support, this attack nonetheless involved twenty thousand rebels—a much larger undertaking than the more famous Pickett-Pettigrew-Trimble Charge at Gettysburg. It was a colossal failure. While Hood suffered over six thousand Confederate casualties, the worst result for him was the loss of over sixty virtually irreplaceable division, brigade, and regimental commanders.[17]

Hood believed that he could not retreat because of the negative effect that would have on morale; therefore, following Schofield's troops, he advanced to the Nashville area and laid a mini siege to the city. Thomas built up his command and assaulted Hood when good weather returned in mid-December. The rebel commander managed to defend his position on the fifteenth and regrouped that evening. However, the next day the Union troops overran Hood's defenses, routing his army. After a miserable retreat back to Tupelo, Mississippi, covered by Maj. Gen. Nathan B. Forrest's cavalry, Hood resigned. The Army of Tennessee, reduced to some eighteen thousand men, had been virtually eliminated as a combat force. Many of the remaining soldiers were granted furloughs, never to return to the army.[18]

During Sherman's March to the Sea, Federals crossed central Georgia, destroyed anything of military value, lived off the land, and displayed the ability to march at will anywhere in the southern Confederacy. After a brief fight, Sherman captured Savannah, Georgia, and presented the city to Lincoln as a Christmas present.[19]

The Union commander convinced Grant that it would be better if his army marched up the East Coast rather than sailed in order to combine forces with him in Virginia, where he laid siege to Lee's army around Petersburg. Marching north, Sherman's men were especially tough on the inhabitants of South Carolina, the initial seat of secession, leaving much of that state in desolation.[20]

Grant was finally able to break through Lee's lines on April 2, 1865, forcing Lee and the Army of Northern Virginia to abandon Richmond. Lee and his army fled west with Grant in hot pursuit. Finally surrounded, the Confederate commander surrendered what was left of the Army of Northern Virginia at Appomattox Court House on April 9.[21]

Gen. Joseph E. Johnston, placed in command of most of the rest of the Confederates in the East, and assisted by the remnants of the Army of Tennessee, was unable to halt Sherman's advance. Upon confirming that Lee had surrendered, Johnston resolved to do the same. After meeting with Sherman several times, and after adjustments demanded by the US War Department were made, Johnston surrendered on April 26. The Civil War was effectively over.[22]

The assassination of President Lincoln on April 14 created a pall over the Union and changed the path of Reconstruction. Confederate president Davis was captured and incarcerated. The Union had finally achieved victory, while the former Confederate states could slowly begin to return to some semblance of normal. The Civil War had run its course.[23]

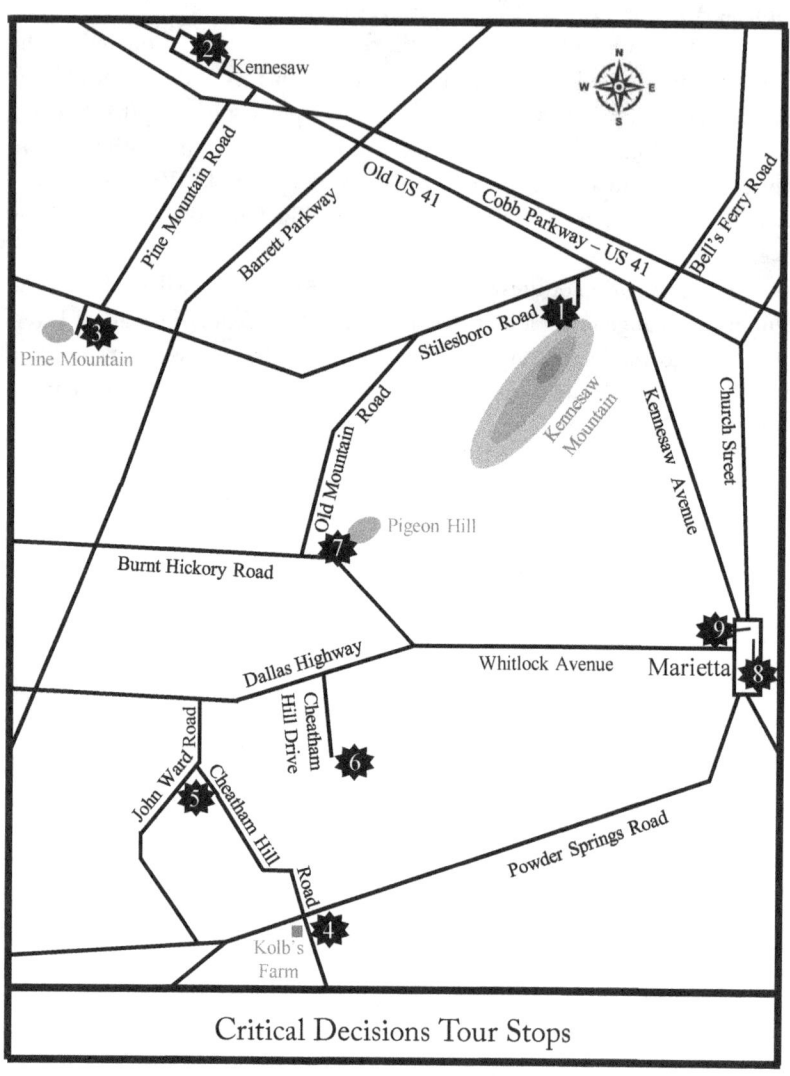

Critical Decisions Tour Stops

APPENDIX I

DRIVING TOUR OF THE CRITICAL DECISIONS OF THE BATTLE OF KENNESAW MOUNTAIN

This driving tour of the critical decisions of the Battle of Kennesaw Mountain brings readers to locations where many of those decisions were made. What follows is not specifically a tour of the battle or battlefield, although it certainly covers much of it. We encourage readers to deviate from this tour when necessary to study other aspects of the battle. The nine stops on this journey are generally in chronological order.

Please drive safely, and either read about each stop and directions to it while parked, or have a passenger read the related materials. Park safely out of traffic, and walk carefully as necessary. Also, please note that Kennesaw Mountain National Battlefield Park (NBP) is one of only a few green spaces around Marietta and Kennesaw. As such, it is heavily visited, especially on weekends, not particularly by students of the Civil War, and parking is usually at a premium. If your schedule permits, plan to take this tour during the week and avoid weekends.

The driving tour starts at the Kennesaw Mountain NBP visitor center, located at 900 Kennesaw Mountain Drive in Kennesaw, Georgia, just west of Marietta. From I-75 take Exit 269, and go west on the Barrett Parkway 2.1 miles to the intersection with Old Highway 41. Turn left (southeast) onto Old

Appendix I

Highway 41, and continue 1.2 miles to the intersection with Stilesboro Road. Turn right (southwest) onto Stilesboro Road, and almost immediately, in 100 yards, turn left (southeast) into the Kennesaw Mountain NBP visitor center parking lot. Park, and explore the visitor center if open. Note that an overflow parking lot is available if necessary.

Stop 1: Kennesaw Mountain National Battlefield Park Visitor Center

Critical Decisions: (1) Johnston Abandons the Mud Creek Line and Retreats to the Kennesaw Mountain Line, (5) Confederate Artillery Is Dragged to the Top of Big and Little Kennesaw Mountains

Maps, books, a small museum, additional information, and restrooms are located here. For hours and days of operation of the visitor center, call 770-

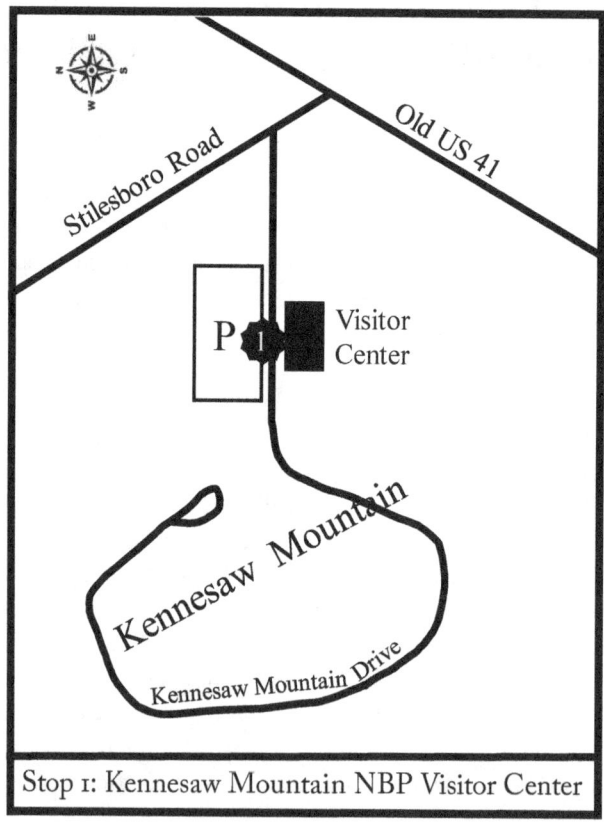

Stop 1: Kennesaw Mountain NBP Visitor Center

Driving Tour of the Critical Decisions of the Battle of Kennesaw Mountain

Visitor Center, Kennesaw Mountain National Battlefield Park. Courtesy of Bill Gurry.

427-4686, extension 0, or visit NPS.gov/KEMO. At the time of this book's publication, you can drive to the top of Kennesaw Mountain in your vehicle during the week, but you must ride the park shuttle on the weekend. The view from the top on a clear day is spectacular. While in the area, read the following account of the battle:

Narrative of Gen. Joseph E. Johnston, CSA, Commanding Department and Army of Tennessee

On the 16th a new disposition was made on the left. Hardee's corps changed front to the rear on its right, by which it was placed on the high ground east of Mud Creek, facing to the west. The right of the Federal army made a corresponding movement, and approached Hardee's line, opposed in advancing by Jackson's division, as well as twenty-five hundred men can contend with twenty-five thousand.

This disposition made an angle where Hardee's right joined Loring's left, which was soon found to be a great defect, for it exposed the troops near it to annoyance from enfilade, which should have been foreseen. Another position, including the crest of Kenesaw [*sic*], was chosen on the 17th and prepared for occupation under the direction of Colonel Prestman [*sic*]. The troops were placed

> on this line on the 19th: Hood's corps massed between the railroad and that from Marietta to Canton; Loring's with a division (his own commanded by Featherstone) between the railroad and eastern base of the mountain, and Walthall's and French's along the crest of the short ridge—French's left reaching its southwestern base, and Hardee's from French's left almost due south across the Lost Mountain and Marietta road, to the brow of the high ground immediately north of the branch of Nose's [Noyes] Creek that runs from Marietta—Walker's division on the right, Bate's next, then Cleburne's, and Cheatham's on the left.[1]

When ready, depart the visitor center to Tour Stop 2, about 4 miles northwest of here—the Kennesaw (Big Shanty at the time) railroad station and the Southern Museum of Civil War and Locomotive History, located at 2898 Cherokee Street NW in downtown Kennesaw, Georgia, next to the railroad. Depart the visitor center, turning right (northeast) onto Stilesboro Road NW. Immediately move to the left turn lane at the stoplight at the junction with Old Highway 41. Turn left (northwest) onto Old Highway 41, and drive about 4 miles into downtown Kennesaw, where Old Highway 41 becomes Main Street. At the intersection with Cherokee Street, after traveling 3.8 miles, turn right (east) onto Cherokee Street, and cross the two sets of railroad tracks. Park in the museum's parking lot on your left (north), the south parking lot on your right, or nearby. Leave your vehicle, and face west toward the railroad tracks. (Visiting the museum is strictly optional, although very informative. The restored railroad engine the *General* is located inside. For museum hours and days of operation, call 770-427-2117 or visit southernmuseum.org.) Carefully cross the railroad tracks, and observe the interpretive markers in the small park just west of the museum. Also observe the old railroad depot just south of the museum.

Stop 2: The Western and Atlantic Railroad Depot (and the Southern Museum of Civil War and Locomotive History)

Critical Decision: (1) Johnston Abandons the Mud Creek Line and Retreats to the Kennesaw Mountain Line

This location is on the original site of the Western and Atlantic Railroad, which both Maj. Gen. William T. Sherman and Gen. Joseph E. Johnston depended on for supplies. Sherman tried to leave the railroad in order to

Driving Tour of the Critical Decisions of the Battle of Kennesaw Mountain

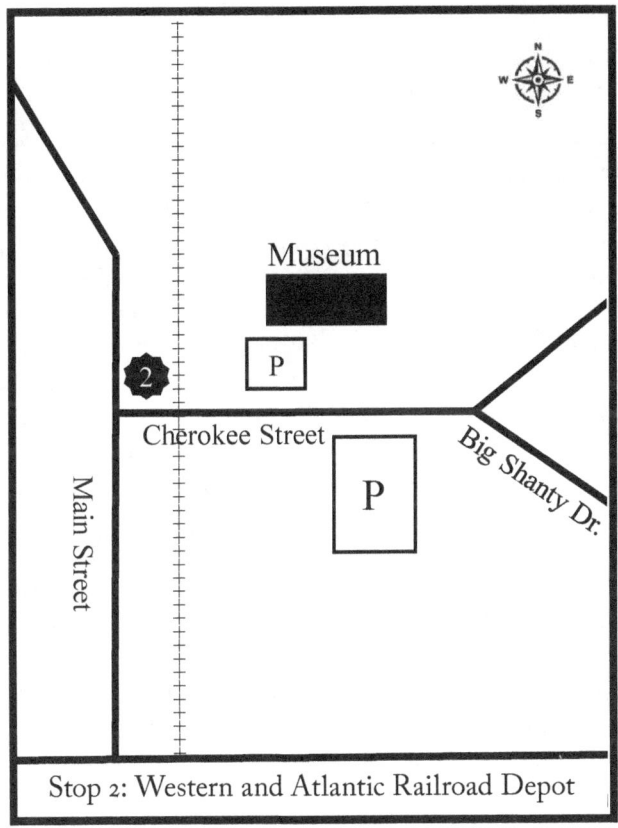

outflank Johnston, resulting in the Hell Hole fighting in and around New Hope, Dallas, and Pickett's Mill. However, the Federal commander quickly realized he could not leave the railroad, as he continuously required supplies that reached him via that route. This site is representative of the railroad and is located near the north end of Sherman's line around Kennesaw, labeled Big Shanty at the time, where Union troops drew supplies from incoming trains. The Great Locomotive Chase of 1862, which featured the locomotive *General*, began at the station here. Across the tracks (west) was the location of Confederate Camp McDonald, a training site for new enlistees.[2]

Sherman continued to advance southward toward Atlanta, but he was now fully committed to protecting his railroad supply line. He had calculated that he needed 130 boxcars' worth of supplies per day to subsist his armies.

Narrative of Maj. Gen. William T. Sherman, USA, Commanding Military Division of the Mississippi

We could not attempt an advance into Georgia without food, ammunition, etc.; and ordinary prudence dictated that we should have an accumulation at the front, in case of interruption to the railway by the act of the enemy, or by common accident. Accordingly, on the 6th of April, I issued a general order, limiting the use of the railroad-cars to transporting only the essential articles of food, ammunition, and supplies for the army proper, forbidding any further issues to citizens, and cutting off all civil traffic; requiring the commanders of posts within thirty miles of Nashville to haul out their own stores in wagons; requiring all troops destined for the front to march, and all beef-cattle to be driven on their own legs. This was a great help, but of course it naturally raised a howl. Some of the poor people of East Tennessee appealed to President Lincoln, whose kind heart responded promptly to their request. He telegraphed me to know if I could not modify or repeal my orders; but I answered him that a great campaign was impending, on which the fate of the nation hung; that our railroads had but a limited capacity, and could not provide for the necessities of the army and of the people too; that one or the other must quit, and we could not until the army of Jos. Johnston was conquered, etc., etc. Mr. Lincoln seemed to acquiesce, and I advised the people to obtain and drive out cattle from Kentucky, and to haul out their supplies by the wagon-road from the same quarter, by way of Cumberland Gap. By these changes I nearly or quite doubled our daily accumulation of stores at the front, and yet even this was not found enough.

I accordingly called together in Nashville the master of transportation, Colonel Anderson, the chief quartermaster, General J. L. Donaldson, and the chief commissary, General Amos Beckwith, for conference. I assumed the strength of the army to move from Chattanooga into Georgia at one hundred thousand men, and the number of animals to be fed, for both cavalry and draught, at thirty-five thousand; then, allowing for occasional wrecks of trains, which were very common, and for the interruption of the road itself by guerrillas and regular raids, we estimated that it would require one hundred and thirty cars, of ten tons each, to reach Chattanooga daily, to be reasonably certain of an adequate supply. Even with this calculation, we could not afford to bring forward hay for the horses and mules, nor more than five pounds of oats or corn per day for each animal. I was willing to risk the question of forage in part, because I expected to find wheat and corn fields, and a good deal of grass, as we advanced into Georgia at that season of the year. The problem then was to deliver at Chattanooga and beyond one hundred and thirty car-loads daily, leaving the beef-cattle to be driven on the hoof, and all the troops in excess of the usual train-guards to march by the ordinary roads. . . .

. . . On the 15th [of June] we advanced our general lines, intending to attack at any weak point discovered between Kennesaw and Pine Mountain; but Pine Mountain was found to be abandoned, and Johnston had contracted his front somewhat, on a direct line connecting Kennesaw with Lost Mountain. Thomas and Schofield thereby gained about two miles of most difficult country, and McPherson's left lapped well around the north end of Kennesaw. We captured a good many prisoners, among them a whole infantry regiment, the Fourteenth Alabama, three hundred and twenty strong.

On the 16th the general movement was continued, when Lost Mountain was abandoned by the enemy. Our right naturally swung around, so as to threaten the railroad below Marietta, but Johnston had still further contracted and strengthened his lines, covering Marietta and all the roads below.[3]

Tour Stop 3 is the summit of Pine Mountain, located about 4 miles southeast. Leave the area of the museum, driving west across the railroad tracks back to South Main Street. Turn left (southeast) onto South Main Street, and then turn right (west) onto Watts Drive. Proceed west on Watts Drive 0.4 mile to the Cobb Parkway / US 41. Turn slightly right (northwest) onto the Cobb Parkway, and immediately maneuver into the left lane to turn left (south) at the next intersection with Pine Mountain Road. Turn left, and proceed south and southwest on Pine Mountain Road about 2.0 miles to the intersection with Stilesboro Road NW. Turn right (west) onto Stilesboro Road NW, and then immediately, in 0.1 mile, turn left onto Beaumont Drive. Continue 0.6 mile past a couple of large storage tanks on the left to the top of Pine Mountain (approximate address 1436 Beaumont Drive). Carefully turn around so that your vehicle faces north, and park on the shoulder by the

Appendix I

marker entitled "Pine Mountain." Walk west to the fenced-in area with a monument to Polk. Please note that this is located on private property. The owner allows visitors, but please be respectful.

Stop 3: Pine Mountain

Critical Decision: (1) Johnston Abandons the Mud Creek Line and Retreats to the Kennesaw Mountain Line

The Confederate Lost Mountain Line ran from Lost Mountain on the west to Brushy Mountain on the east, including the Pine Mountain salient, which extended north from the main rebel line. Concerned about the formation's vulnerability, Hardee requested that Johnston evaluate the wisdom of having Maj. Gen. William B. Bate's division remain on the mountain. The next morning, June 14, corps commanders Polk and Hardee accompanied Johnston to the summit. Although advised not to show themselves, they nevertheless did. Sherman happened to observe them and ordered the nearby Fifth Indiana Light Battery to open fire, which it did, killing Polk. After Federal assaults on the salient that day, Johnston directed Bate to withdraw

Pine Mountain, Kennesaw, GA. Photo by the author.

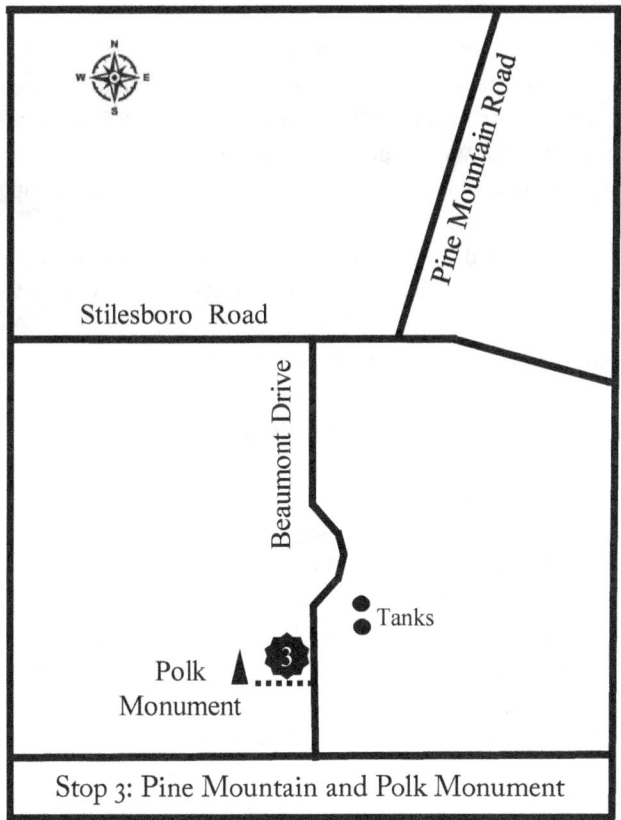

Stop 3: Pine Mountain and Polk Monument

that evening. Further Union attacks on the fifteenth and sixteenth forced Johnston to consolidate his extended line into the new Mud Creek Line running just east of Mud Creek facing west. Unfortunately for the rebels, the line turned right near the Latimer House, creating another exposed salient. By the eighteenth Johnston realized the vulnerability of this location, and he retreated that evening to the Kennesaw Mountain Line.[4]

Narrative of Richard McMurry, *Atlanta 1864: Last Chance for the Confederacy*

By then cavalry reconnaissance had revealed that the Rebels were present in force in the front and holding a fortified line stretching from the railroad southwest as far as Lost Mountain.

Soon after beginning their advance, the Yankees ran into Confederate skirmishers. Over the next several days small-scale fighting erupted here and there along the line of contact between opposing forces, but there was no general engagement. Sherman's attention soon focused on Pine Mountain, which stood a short distance in advance of the Secessionists' line.

Johnston had posted William B. Bate's division of Hardee's Corps in the forward position on Pine Mountain and had connected that outpost to the rest of the Rebel works with a network of trenches. Pine Mountain thus became a salient, or projecting angle, in the Confederate line. A Rebel punster quipped that Johnston was setting a trap for Sherman, using the troops on Pine Mountain as the "bate."

By June 12 Thomas had the Army of the Cumberland deployed in front of the Pine Mountain salient, and Sherman had realized that he might break Johnston's line by thrusting some of his force in between Pine and Kennesaw Mountains. On that and the following day Thomas worked his army around to the east of Pine Mountain, and it appeared that the Yankees might isolate Bate's Division, cutting it off from the rest of the Rebel Army.

On the morning of June 14 Johnston and Hardee went to Pine Mountain to study the salient and decide if they should withdraw Bate's troops from so endangered a post. Polk accompanied them to avail himself of the height to study the ground in front of his own line to the east. Foolishly disregarding warnings that the Yankee artillery had the exact range of the mountaintop, the generals climbed onto the breastworks to get a clear view of the area below. A large group of Bate's soldiers soon gathered to watch the high-ranking officers.

Sherman too, was out on the lines that morning. When he observed a crowd of Rebels on the summit of Pine Mountain, he ordered nearby artillery to disperse the group with a few shots. The Confederate generals had just begun to walk away from the summit when the first round fell near them. Quickly the group scurried for cover, and all but Polk soon reached places of safety. The Bishop-general did not want to set a bad example for the men. As he walked deliberately away from the exposed area, something attracted his attention, and he stopped for a better look. As he did, a cannonball passed through his body. He was the second highest-ranking Confederate killed in the war (after Gen. Albert Sidney Johnston, who died at Shiloh April 6, 1862).

. . . The weak part of the position was the left, and on June 16 some of Schofield's troops, moving around to the south on the far right of Sherman's front, seized high ground from which their artillery could enfilade Hardee's line off to the east.

Schofield's success forced Hardee to reposition his corps. That night, therefore, he abandoned much of his line and pulled his left back to a ridge east of Mud Creek. . . .

On the seventeenth Thomas discovered that the angle in the Confederate line permitted his guns to enfilade Hardee's new position from the north. Obviously the Southerners could not long remain. . . . During the night of June 18–19 Johnston moved his troops back to [the Kennesaw Mountain Line].[5]

Tour Stop 4 is Kolb's Farm, located about 8 miles southeast. Drive north back to the intersection with Stilesboro Road NW. Turn right (east) onto Stilesboro Road NW, and drive 2.0 miles to the intersection with New Salem Road. Turn right (south) onto New Salem Road, and drive 1.4 miles to the intersection with Burnt Hickory Road. Turn left (east) onto Burnt Hickory Road. Proceed less than 0.1 mile to the Barrett Parkway, and turn right (southwest) onto the Barrett Parkway. When able, merge into the left lane. Follow the Barrett Parkway 1.4 miles to the intersection with the Dallas Highway / GA 120. Turn left (east) onto the Dallas Highway, and drive about 1.0 mile to the intersection with John Ward Road on the right (south). Turn right (south) onto John Ward Road. Continue 0.5 mile to the roundabout, and take the second exit onto Cheatham Hill Road. Travel 2.0 miles to the intersection with the Powder Springs Road / GA 360. Cross Powder Springs Road, which becomes Callaway Road SW, and immediately turn right (west) into the Kolb's Farm parking lot. Walk to the interpretive markers. Note that the Kolb House is a private residence; do not trespass.

Stop 4: The Battle of Kolb's Farm

Critical Decisions: (6) Sherman Attempts to Outflank Johnston's Left Flank, (7) Johnston Orders Hood to Protect the Left Flank, (8) Hood Orders an Attack on the Newly Deployed Union Right Flank

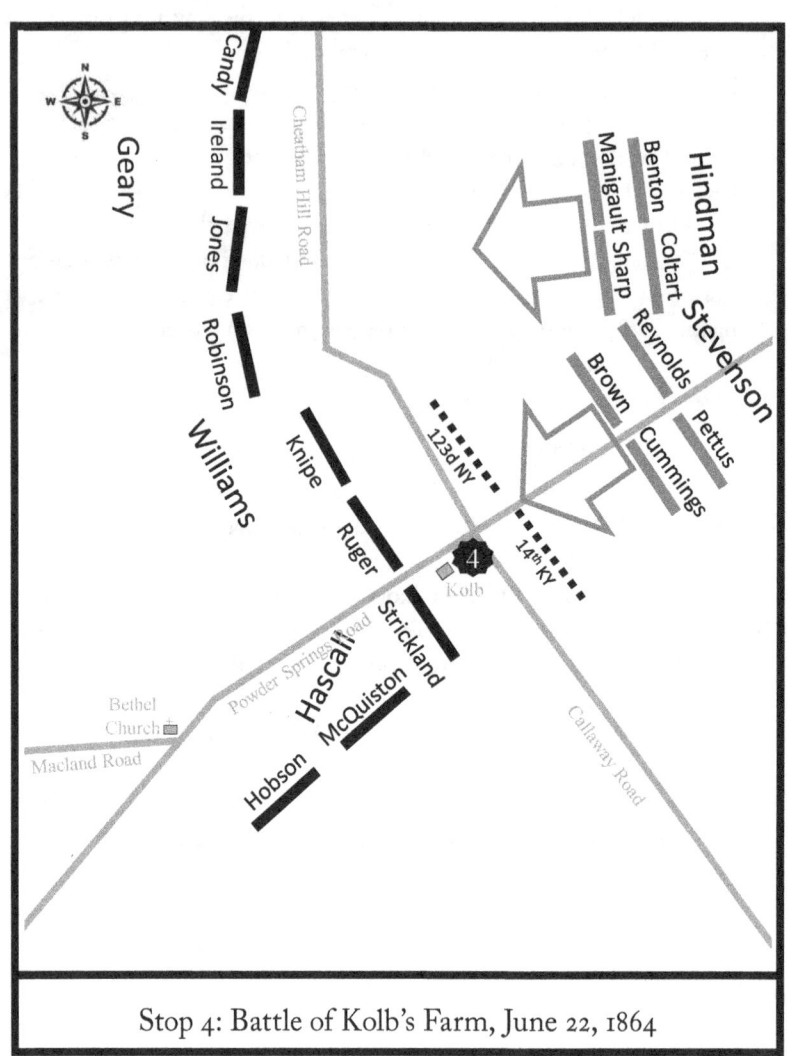

Stop 4: Battle of Kolb's Farm, June 22, 1864

Driving Tour of the Critical Decisions of the Battle of Kennesaw Mountain

Kolb's Farm, Kennesaw Mountain National Battlefield Park. Photo by the author.

On the late afternoon of June 22, Lieut. Gen. John B. Hood ordered an attack on the Union left without coordinating with his commander or obtaining permission to do so. Since Hood only devoted two paragraphs to the Kennesaw Mountain fighting in his memoirs, we don't know of his motivation to conduct this battle. Perhaps he desired to show he was an aggressive commander and attempt to turn the Union right flank. His attack failed, costing the Confederacy over one thousand casualties, compared with about three hundred Federal soldiers. Initially, Johnston believed Hood's report of repealing an attack by two Union regiments, but he later changed his mind, as indicated in this narrative below.[6]

Narrative of William R. Scaife, *The Campaign for Atlanta*

Hood made little, if any, reconnaissance to determine the position or strength of the enemy or the nature of the terrain to his front. Then, without consultation with his commanding officer, Joseph E. Johnston, he ordered an all out assault which would commit a third of the army in a large, unauthorized battle. Carter L. Stevenson's division was ordered to move diagonally across the Powder Springs Road to attack the Federal center, which was manned by Hascall's division and four batteries of artillery. Thomas C. Hindman's division

Appendix I

was ordered to advance on Stevenson's right, through the ravines cut by Ward's Creek and its tributaries and into the gap between Hascall's and William's divisions. . . .

On the right, Hindman advanced through deep ravines into the gap between Geary's and Hascall's divisions and was caught by an enfilading crossfire from both sides. Unable to find cover in the marsh of Ward's Creek, Hindman pulled back several hundred yards into the woods near the Camp House and removed his division from the battle. . . . Late in the day, Hood ordered Alex P. Stewart's division to advance on the extreme left, near the Widow Kolb House, but it was only lightly engaged and soon retired.[7]

Report of Maj. Gen. Carter L. Stevenson, CSA, Commanding Stevenson's Division, Hood's Corps, Army of Tennessee

My division had for one or two days previous to the 22d of June been lying in reserve on the extreme left of the infantry of the army, about three miles from Marietta, on the Powder Springs road. About 12 p.m. I moved the command farther from Marietta and halted it at Mount Zion Church. The enemy, as I moved forward, were driving in the cavalry. About 2.30 p.m. I was directed to take position on the left of General Hindman's division, about half a mile in advance of the church. I at once advanced my skirmishers, and, driving those of the enemy, established my line under fire of his artillery. Brown's and Cumming's brigades formed the first line, Reynolds' and Pettus' the second, the men hastily constructed breast-works of logs and rails. Soon afterwards I received orders to advance from my position and drive the enemy on the road toward Manning's Mill. The division of General Hindman was also directed to advance on my right. I placed General Cumming in charge of the first line—Brown's and Cumming's brigades, commanded by Cols. Ed. C. Cook (Thirty-second Tennessee) and E. P. Watkins (Fifty-sixth Georgia), respectively, and General Pettus in charge of the second line—Reynolds' and Pettus' brigades, commanded by Cols. R. C. Trigg (Fifty-fourth Virginia) and C. M. Shelley (Thirtieth Alabama), respectively. A good deal of time was occupied in getting and giving instructions and making the necessary preparations. About 5 p.m. we advanced and soon struck the enemy, driving him quickly before us from his advanced works, which consisted of one line of logs and rail works complete, and one partially constructed. The fire under which this was done was exceedingly heavy, and the artillery of the enemy, which was massed in large force and admirably posted, was served with a rapidity and fatal precision which could not be surpassed. The nature of the ground over which we passed was most unfavorable to such a movement—the two right brigades moved for much of the way over open fields, the two left through dense undergrowth. The line thus became more irregular and broken every moment, and when the two right brigades had driven the enemy into their main works the line was so much broken and mixed up that, although the men were in good spirits and perfectly willing to make the attempt, it was not deemed practicable to carry the works by assault. The commands were halted and the best possible line, under the circumstances, formed. Brown's and Trigg's (Reynolds') brigades lay in a swampy ravine within pistol-shot of the enemy's works; the other two brigades held the road on their left. The dead and wounded were all removed to the rear, and after holding our position for several hours, in compliance with the orders of General Hood, the division returned to its old position. With perhaps some few exceptions the conduct of the troops was highly creditable.

My loss was heavy—807 killed and wounded.[8]

Narrative of Gen. Joseph E. Johnston, CSA, Commanding Department and Army of Tennessee

As the extension of the Federal army toward the Chattahoochee made a corresponding one necessary on our part, Hood's corps was transferred from the right to the Powder-Spring road, his right near and south of Cheatham's left. General Hood was instructed to endeavor to prevent any progress of the Federal right toward the railroad; the course of which was nearly parallel to our left and centre. Our position, consequently, was a very hazardous one.

Next day [June 22] a sharp but brief fire of musketry on the left, succeeded by that of, apparently, several batteries, announced that Hood's corps, or a large part of it, was engaged. Soon after the firing ceased, General Hood reported that Hindman's and Stevenson's divisions of his corps had been attacked, and that they had not only

> repulsed the enemy, but had followed them to a line of light intrenchments and driven them from it; but that, being exposed, in this position, to a fire of intrenched artillery, they had been compelled to withdraw.
>
> Subsequent and more minute accounts of this affair, by general and staff officers of the corps, converted the favorable impression made by this report into the belief that, instead of achieving success, we had suffered a reverse. It appeared that our troops had not fallen back merely to escape annoyance, but that, after the Federal infantry had been driven back to and then beyond its line of breastworks, Lieutenant-General Hood determined to capture the intrenched artillery referred to in his brief report. It crowned a high, bare hill, facing the interval between his right and the left of Hardee's corps. To direct his line toward it, a partial change of front to the right was necessary, and that slow operation, performed under the fire of a formidable artillery, subjected his two divisions to a loss so severe that the attempt was soon abandoned—I am uncertain whether by the decision of the commander, or the discretion of the troops themselves; not, however, until they had lost about a thousand men.[9]

Tour Stop 5 is the site of Sherman's (and Thomas's) headquarters, which you passed on the way to Kolb's Farm, located about two miles north. Return to the intersection of Powder Springs Road and Callaway Road. Cross the intersection and continue north on Cheatham Hill Road, backtracking the route you took to reach Kolb's Farm, for 1.7 miles, and turn left (west) into the parking area which was the site of Sherman's Headquarters. Park, walk to, and read the interpretive sign and historical markers. Note that the site of Thomas's headquarters is at the south end of the parking lot.

Stops 5A and 5B: Sherman's Headquarters

Critical Decisions: (9) Sherman Orders an Assault on the Center of the Kennesaw Mountain Line, (11) Sherman Outflanks Johnston to Advance Toward the Chattahoochee River

Stop 5A

Face east, the direction of the assault that began here. Sherman grew tired of continually having to outflank Johnston without actually confronting him, even though he had advanced many miles into Georgia. He believed that

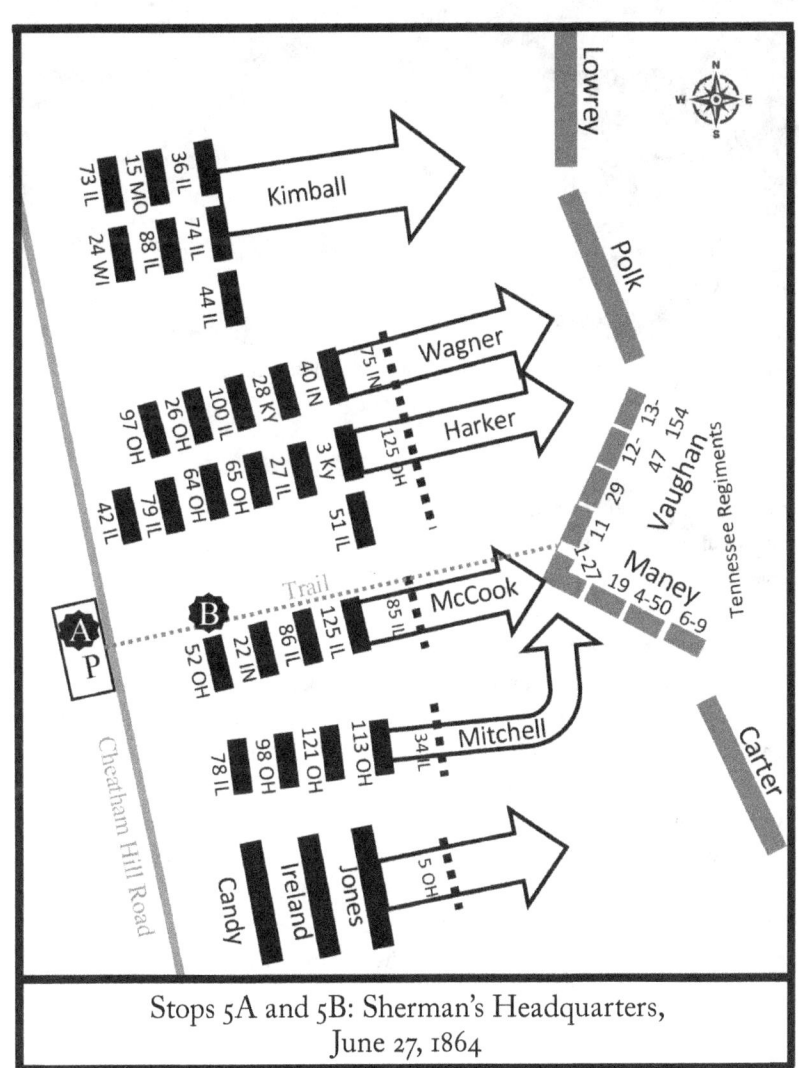

Stops 5A and 5B: Sherman's Headquarters, June 27, 1864

Sherman's Headquarters, Kennesaw Mountain National Battlefield Park. Courtesy of Bill Gurry.

Johnston had been forced to stretch his line over some seven miles to protect his flanks, and therefore his center might be weak and vulnerable to an assault. Sherman ordered an assault to take place on June 27. Fortunately for the rebels, it failed.

You have two options here. The better choice, if everyone is physically able, is to walk the same ground east of the headquarters area as the Union assault forces did—down and across the branch of John Ward Creek, then up to the Dead Angle and Illinois Monument on Cheatham Hill, which is the next tour stop. This assault trail is less than a half mile long, and it typically takes less than fifteen minutes to travel for those in good physical condition. If someone in your party can drive to the Cheatham Hill parking lot, you can meet there. Otherwise, you will have to retrace your route to Sherman's Headquarters parking lot. The advantage of these options is that you will appreciate more than ever the value of the terrain involved, and the incredible odds against the Union assaulting force. If you prefer, you can leave this location, drive to Cheatham Hill, and view the assault and terrain involved from the Dead Angle there.

Narrative of Maj. Gen. William T. Sherman, USA, Commanding Military Division of the Mississippi

During the 24th and 25th of June General Schofield extended his right as far as prudent, so as to compel to thin out his lines correspondingly, with the intention to make two strong assaults at points where success would give us the greatest advantage. I had consulted Generals Thomas, McPherson, and Schofield, and we all agreed that we could not with prudence stretch out any more, and therefore there was no alternative but to attack "fortified lines," a thing carefully avoided up to that time. I reasoned, if we could make a breach anywhere near the rebel centre, and thrust in a strong head of column, that with the one moiety [part or share] of our army we could hold in check the corresponding wing of the enemy, and with the other sweep in flank and overwhelm the other half. The 27th of June was fixed as the day for the attempt, and in order to oversee the whole, and to be in close communication with all parts of the army, I had a place cleared on the top of a hill to the rear of Thomas's centre, and had telegraph-wires laid to it. The points of attack were chosen, and the troops were all prepared with as little demonstration as possible. About 9 a.m. of the day appointed, the troops moved to the assault, and all along our lines for ten miles a furious fire of artillery and musketry was kept up. At all points the enemy met us with determined courage and in great force. McPherson's attacking column fought up the face of the lesser Kenesaw [sic], but could not reach the summit. About a mile to the right (just below the Dallas road) Thomas's assaulting column reached the parapet where Brigadier-General Harker was shot down mortally wounded, and Brigadier-General Daniel McCook (my old law partner) was desperately wounded, from the effects of which he afterward died. By 11:30 the assault was in fact over, and had failed. We had not broken the rebel line at either point, but our assaulting columns held their ground within a few yards of the rebel trenches, and there covered themselves with parapet. McPherson lost about five hundred men and several valuable officers, and Thomas lost nearly two thousand men. This was the hardest fight of the campaign up to that date, and it is well described by Johnston in his "Narrative" (pages 342, 343), where he admits his loss in killed and wounded as—Hood's corps (not reported), Hardee's corps—286, Loring's (Polk's)—522, Total 808.

> This, no doubt is a true and fair statement; but, as usual, Johnston overestimates our loss, putting it at six thousand, whereas our entire loss was about twenty-five hundred, killed and wounded.[10]
>
> ### Narrative of Gen. Joseph E. Johnston, CSA, Commanding Department and Army of Tennessee
>
> I think that the estimate of Northern officers of their killed and wounded on that occasion, "near three thousand," does great injustice to the character of General Sherman's army. Such a loss, in the large force that must have been furnished for a decisive and general attack by an army of almost a hundred thousand men, would have been utterly insignificant—too trifling to discourage, much less defeat brave soldiers, such as composed General Sherman's army. It does injustice to Southern marksmanship, too. The fire of twenty thousand infantry inured to battle, and intrenched, and of fifty field pieces poured into such columns, frequently with pistol-shot, must have done much greater execution.[11]

Typically, for every soldier killed in battle during the Civil War, five were wounded. As Johnston implies, the Union total perhaps should have been closer to six thousand casualties.[12]

If desired, walk to the south end of the parking lot and visit the site of Thomas's headquarters. When ready, carefully cross Cheatham Hill Road, and walk about 100 yards east on the designated pathway. Stop and face east.

Stop 5B

Regardless of whether you hike the assault trail to the Dead Angle on Cheatham Hill, a tradition is for you or someone in your party to repeat Col. Dan McCook's supposed recitation of the twenty-seventh verse of Thomas B. Macaulay's "Horatius." Although some doubt that McCook recited this verse to motivate his men just before the assault, the poem nonetheless sets the tone for what happened. Macaulay translated the verse from the Latin text concerning Publius Horatius Cocles, a famous commander who defended the Sublician Bridge over the Tiber River from the advancing Etruscan army.[13]

"Horatius"

> Then out spake brave Horatius,

Driving Tour of the Critical Decisions of the Battle of Kennesaw Mountain

Thomas's Headquarters, Kennesaw Mountain National Battlefield Park. Courtesy of Bill Gurry.

The Captain of the gate:
"To every man upon this earth
Death cometh soon or late
And how can man die better
Than facing fearful odds,
For the ashes of his fathers
And the temples of his Gods."[14]

If you hiked to the Dead Angle on Cheatham Hill and explored it, you can skip directions to the next stop as you are already there. Otherwise, the next stop is Cheatham Hill, which is only 0.5 mile east of your current location but involves several miles of driving to reach. Leave the headquarters parking lot, turn left (north), and proceed about 0.2 mile to the roundabout. Take the first exit onto John Ward Road, and continue 0.5 mile north to the Dallas Highway / GA 120. Turn right (east) onto the Dallas Highway, which becomes Whitlock Avenue NW, and travel 0.4 mile, passing by the Old John Ward Road turnoff on your right. Turn right onto Cheatham Hill Drive, and continue about 0.6 mile to the Cheatham Hill parking lot. Park, visit the interpretive markers there, and then follow the trail south some 200 yards to the Dead Angle and the Illinois Monument. Face west, and examine the steep terrain sloping down in that direction.

Appendix I

Stop 6: Cheatham Hill / Dead Angle

Critical Decisions: (3) Confederate Engineers Use the Topographical Crest Instead of the Military Crest, (4) Cheatham Carefully Locates and Camouflages His Artillery, (9) Sherman Orders an Assault on the Center of the Kennesaw Mountain Line, (10) Union Commanders Assault Using Columns of Brigades

As you examine the terrain sloping up to the Dead Angle, and to Maney's and Vaughan's entrenchments located here, you cannot help but be impressed by the courage the Union soldiers displayed in charging these works. Likewise, the bravery of the comparatively few Confederate soldiers of these two brigades in holding back the assault becomes even more obvious. As historian Earl Hess notes, most of the fighting that took place here, just in front of the Dead Angle, was conducted within no more than a couple of thousand square feet, with some four thousand Yankees attacking as few as one thousand rebels.[15]

Unfortunately for the Confederates manning the Dead Angle, rebel engineers ignored the military crest when laying out the defensive line on Cheatham Hill. This proved extremely problematic for the defenders stationed there, Maney's and Vaughan's men.

Narrative of Earl J. Hess, *Fighting for Atlanta: Tactics, Terrain, and Trenches in the Civil War*

The weakest point of Johnston's Kennesaw Line proved to be a sharp salient held by Cheatham's Division of Hardee's Corps. Cheatham was ordered to prolong Cleburne's Division line on June 19 and sent Brig. Gen. Alfred J. Vaughan's Tennessee Brigade to do so. . . .

There was nothing Cheatham could do but adjust to the difficult segment of his line. Yet, when the light of day dawned on June 21, he realized that the trench was ill placed to protect the rise of ground just north of the branch that would become known as Cheatham's [sic] Hill. The engineers had staked out the line in the dark and did not realize that it was placed a bit too far back from the military crest of the slope. The men could not see more than sixty or seventy-five yards ahead before the ground sloped off into another branch of John Ward Creek that ran roughly parallel to the Confederate line. There was, in short, a certain amount of "dead space" in front of Cheatham's [sic] Hill not adequately seen or covered by the defender. Union guns already were playing on the position, so

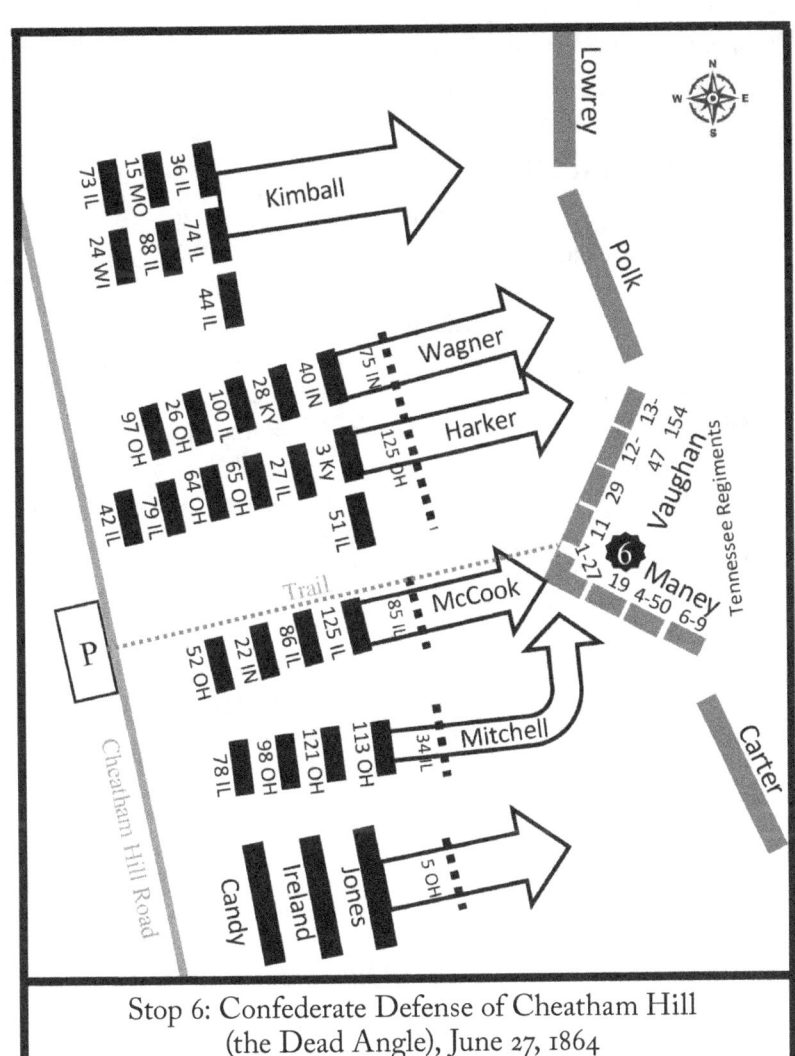

Stop 6: Confederate Defense of Cheatham Hill (the Dead Angle), June 27, 1864

> Cheatham did not feel comfortable ordering his men to adjust the line forward.[16]

The use of columns of brigades, considered a shrewd tactic, failed at Kennesaw Mountain.

> ### Narrative of Earl J. Hess, *Kennesaw Mountain: Sherman, Johnston, and the Atlanta Campaign*
>
> [Col.] John K. Shellenberger argued that forming the brigade in such a long, narrow column inside the Union skirmish line had been a mistake.... Newton's division also proved that columns were rarely effective in conducting attacks on strong enemy positions. Shellenberger's comment that a column was like a battering ram well expressed the emotion-laden perception of that particular formation, with the idea that concentrated mass could physically break through a line like a giant hammer. But the reality was far different. The heads of columns easily collapsed when they hit resistance, either causing the rest of the column to collapse too or at least forcing it to a standstill.... In the worst case scenarios, when a column collapsed like an accordion, the danger posed to individuals when the rear lines collided with the forward lines was real and deadly.[17]

Cheatham carefully placed his artillery and kept it hidden from observation by the Union. As a result, it fired deadly rounds during the assault, contributing directly to the Federal repulse.

> ### Narrative of Christopher Losson, *Tennessee's Forgotten Warriors: Frank Cheatham and His Confederate Division*
>
> Cheatham also had the ten guns nearest the salient camouflaged with brush, and strictly forbade those masked guns from replying when Yankee batteries once again probed the Rebel fortifications. ... Cheatham noted later that his cannon blasts struck the Union columns "from within 50 y[ar]ds of my works to their rear which was still in the valley below." Lieutenant Wright's two guns along Vaughan's front also came into action, as did the two left fieldpieces

Driving Tour of the Critical Decisions of the Battle of Kennesaw Mountain

Vaughan's position, the Dead Angle, Cheatham Hill, Kennesaw Mountain National Battlefield Park. Photo by the author.

from Turner's battery. Gaping holes formed in the Union ranks, and Yankees who survived the carnage latter attested to the savage impact of the shells and canister which swept the slope.[18]

The men of Maney's and Vaughan's Brigades successfully repulsed the vigorous Union assault at the Dead Angle. The fighting conducted by both sides was terrific, and bravery abounded. Nonetheless, the rebels held firm, and the Union assault was deemed a failure.

Narrative of Brig. Gen. Alfred J. Vaughan Jr., CSA, Commanding Vaughan's Brigade, Cheatham's Division, Hardee's Corps, Army of Tennessee

In column seven lines deep, with not a cap on the guns of the first two lines, he attempted to storm our position. Never did men march into the very jaws of death with a firmer tread and with more determination than did the Federals to this attack. But they met intrenched infantry, and the concentrated fire of musketry, canister, grapeshot and shell mowed them down at every step. Yet they struggled forward, but every Confederate stood at his post, and in a short time it was more than mortals could stand and they broke and fled.[19]

Narrative of Pvt. Sam Watkins, CSA, Company H, First Tennessee, Maney's Brigade, Cheatham's Division, Hardee's Corps, Army of Tennessee

I had shot one hundred and twenty times that day [June 27]. My gun became so hot that frequently the powder would flash before I could ram home the ball, and I had frequently to exchange my gun for that of a dead comrade.... When the Yankees fell back, and the firing ceased, I never saw so many broken down and exhausted men in my life. I was sick as a horse, and wet with blood and sweat as I could be, and many of our men were vomiting with excessive fatigue, over exhaustion, and sunstroke; our tongues were parched and cracked for water, and our faces blackened with powder and smoke, and our dead and wounded were piled indiscriminately in the trenches. There was not a single man in the company who was not wounded, or had holes shot through his hat and clothing.[20]

The Union assault at the Dead Angle was not a complete failure. Rather than being shot in the back while retreating, some of the Federals took advantage of the military crest, forming a line just below the Dead Angle where rebel fire went over their heads. These troops hung on, and during the following evenings they rotated in and out. They also began to dig a tunnel, planning to blow up the salient.

Report of Lieut. Col. Allen L. Fahnestock, USA, Commanding Eighty-Sixth Illinois, Third Brigade, Second Division, Fourteenth Corps, Army of the Cumberland

On the 25th of June I moved with the brigade to the right about three miles and remained in camp until the 27th of June. Early on this morning I received orders to be ready to move at sunrise, leaving camp and garrison equipage behind. A charge on the rebel center had been ordered. At about 8 a.m. our gallant and brave colonel (Dan. McCook) formed his brigade, my regiment in the second line. The signal guns soon pealed forth their thunder, and in a moment thousands of brave soldiers stood ready to advance on the traitorous foe. The charge was gallantly led, but the works proved too strong to be carried. In this charge my regiment lost 4 commissioned officers wounded (Capts. Frank Hitchcock, Company D; Edward Vanantwerp, Company E (since dead); Lieut. Samuel T. Rogers (A), and Lieut, and Adjt. L. J. Dawdy, wounded and captured), 27 enlisted men killed, 56 wounded, and 11 captured, all wounded except 3. But notwithstanding the rebel works were not carried, the charging column was not repulsed, for it maintained the position gained and fortified from twenty-five to sixty yards from the rebel works. My regiment, with the brigade, remained within twenty-five yards of the rebel works, keeping up an incessant fire until they fell back, on the night of July 2. During the six days we lay so close to the rebel works my regiment lost additional 2 enlisted men killed and 8 wounded.[21]

Narrative of Earl J. Hess, *Kennesaw Mountain: Sherman, Johnston, and the Atlanta Campaign*

Back on Cheatham's [sic] Hill, the opposing lines were close enough to allow the Federals to begin a mine designed to blow up the angle of the confederate [sic] works. The distance was short, and the Yankees could start the underground approach in the side of the hill, just below the shallow military crest that had saved their lives when the attack broke apart on June 27. It was the first and only time in the Civil War that troops belonging to the Army of the Cumberland attempted a mining project. The only men of Sherman's army group which had experience at this unique form of warfare were members of the Army of the Tennessee, who had dug several mines during the course of the siege of Vicksburg. Johnston's Army of Tennessee had no previous experience at either mining or countermining.

Lieutenant Colonel James W. Langley of the 125th Illinois initiated the mine after he helped to push the forward Union line ahead to a distance of only a few yards from the Confederate works on June 28. As the historian of his regiment put it, Langley intended to detonate the mine on July 4 and "usher in the day by one of the grandest pyrotechnic displays that had ever occurred in those parts." Postwar measurement of what was left of the mine indicated Langley started the excavation 105 feet (35 yards) from the main Confederate line. Allen Fahnestock estimated the tunnel was 16 feet underground at its deepest....

Langley's project neared its completion as the Fourth of July loomed on the calendar. By the night of July 2, the gallery was short

Appendix I

of its goal by twenty to thirty feet, and the word was that higher officers had accumulated enough powder to use in it when ready.[22]

The next tour stop is Pigeon Hill, site of a diversionary assault, about 2 miles north as the crow flies. Leave the Cheatham Hill parking lot, and drive north back to the Dallas Highway / Whitlock Avenue NW / GA 120. Turn right (east) onto Whitlock Avenue NW, and continue about 1.1 miles to a left turn at a stoplight onto Burnt Hickory Road NW. Turn left (north), and proceed about 1.2 miles to the intersection with Old Mountain Road on your right (north). Park in the lot on the left (southwest) side of the intersection. Carefully cross Burnt Hickory Road NW, and walk the trail to Pigeon Mountain, which begins at the northeast corner of the intersection. If able, take the trail, rather steep in places, about 265 yards to the interpretive site on Pigeon Mountain. View the interpretive markers, and then continue facing west.

Stop 7: Pigeon Mountain

Critical Decision: (9) Sherman Orders an Assault on the Center of the Kennesaw Mountain Line

While Sherman directed his main assault at the Dead Angle on Cheatham Hill, he also ordered diversionary assaults along much of the rest of his extended line in hopes of fooling Johnston as to his true intention. McPherson's Sixteenth and Seventeenth Corps engaged in heavy skirmishing to hold Loring's Corps in place. Elements of Logan's Fifteenth Corps took part in the main diversionary assault here at Pigeon Hill. While unsuccessful, they nonetheless provided a distraction.

Narrative of Gen. Joseph E. Johnston, CSA, Commanding Department and Army of Tennessee

In the morning of the 27th, after a furious cannonade, the Federal army made a general assault upon the Confederate position, which was received everywhere with firmness, and repelled with a loss to the assailants enormously disproportionate to that which they inflicted. At several points the characteristic fortitude of the Northwestern soldiers held them under a close and destructive fire long after reasonable hope of success was gone. The attack upon Loring's corps was by the Army of the Tennessee; that upon Hardee's by

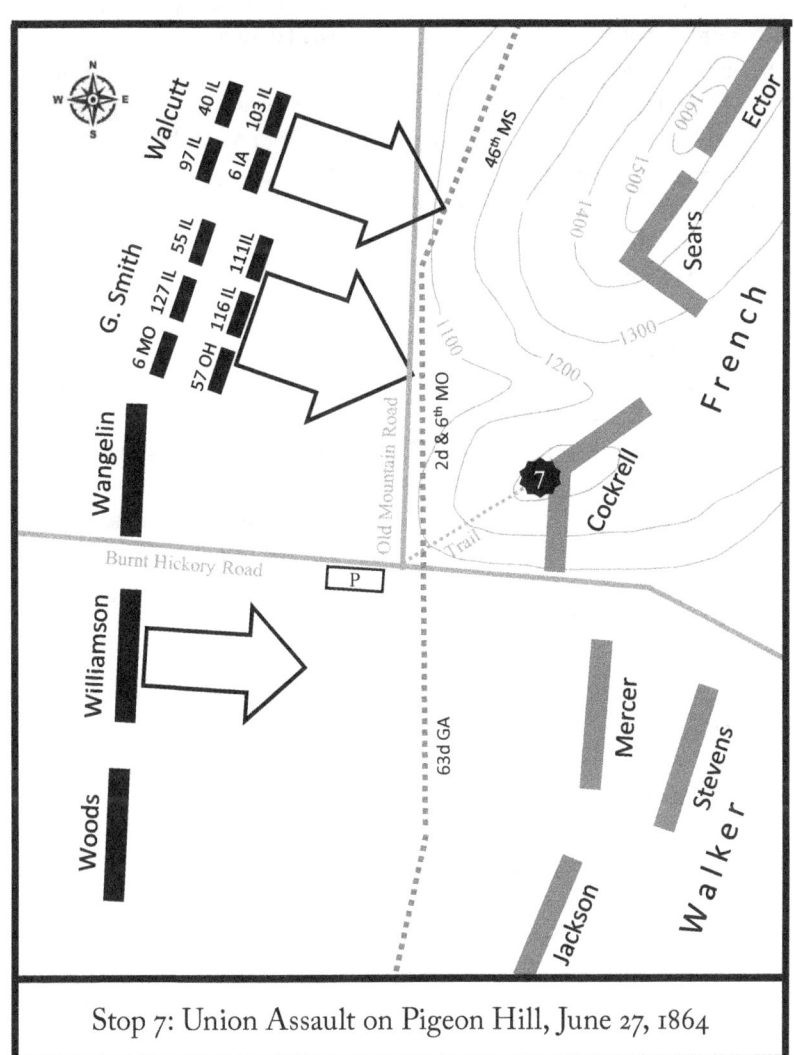

Stop 7: Union Assault on Pigeon Hill, June 27, 1864

the Army of the Cumberland. The principal efforts of the enemy were directed against Loring's right and left brigades, and the left of Hardee's corps.

The attack upon Loring's right—Scott's brigade of Featherstone's division—was by troops of the Seventeenth Corps, advancing in three lines, preceded by skirmishers. They received five or six volleys from Nelson's (Twelfth Louisiana) regiment, deployed as skirmishers, in rifle-pits, six hundred yards in front of the brigade. This regiment held its ground until the first Federal line had approached within twenty-five paces. It then retired to the line of battle. The Federal troops advanced steadily, and two hundred paces from the Confederate line met the fire of Scott's infantry, and received in their flanks that of four batteries. This concentrated fire compelled them to halt. Unable to advance further, and unwilling to retreat, they remained where they had halted almost an hour, before withdrawing from the shower of missiles.

During this time a single line of Federal infantry was engaged with Wheeler's troops, the skirmishers of Featherstone's own, and Adam's brigades, and those of Quarles's brigade of Walthall's division—all in the shelter of rifle-pits. The firing was always within easy, and frequently very short range. A body of the assailants charges into Quarles's rifle-pits, where most of them were killed or captured.

In the assault upon Loring's left (Cockrell's Missouri brigade) the assailants advanced rapidly from the west—their right extending to the south of the Burnt Hickory and Marietta road, and their left encountering the brigade (Sears) on Cockrell's right. Their right dashed through the skirmishers of Walker's right before they could be reinforced, and took in reverse those on the right and left, while they were attacked in front. In a few minutes about eighty of Walker's men had been bayoneted or captured in their rifle-pits. The Federal troops approaching Walker's line on the south of the road were driven back by the fire of artillery directed against their left flank by Major-General French; but the main body, unchecked by Cockrell's skirmishers, pressed forward steadily under the fire of the brigade, until within twenty or thirty paces of its line. Here it was checked and ultimately repulsed, by the steady courage of the Missourians. The action had continued with spirit for about an hour, during most of which time fifty field-pieces were playing upon the Confederate troops.[23]

Narrative of Maj. Gen. Samuel G. French, CSA, Commanding French's Division, Loring's Corps, Army of Tennessee

[June] 27th. This morning there appeared great activity among the Federal staff officers and generals all along my front and up and down the lines. The better to observe what it portended I and my staff seated ourselves on the brow of the [Little Kennesaw] mountain, sheltered by a large rock that rested *between* our guns and those of the enemy, while my infantry line was farther in front, but low down the mountain sides.

Artillery-firing was common at all times on the line, but now it swelled in volume and extended down to the extreme left, and then from fifty guns burst out simultaneously in my front, while battery after battery, following on the right, disclosed a general attack on our entire line. Presently, and as if by magic, there sprang from the earth a host of men, and in one long, waving line of blue the infantry advanced and the battle of Kennesaw Mountain began.

I could see no infantry of the enemy on my immediate front, owing to the woods at the base of the mountain, and therefore directed the guns from their elevated position to enfilade the blue line advancing on Walker's front, in full view. In a short time this flank fire down on their line drove them back, and Walker was relieved from the attack....

Through the rifts of smoke, or as it was wafted aside by the wind, we could see the assault made on Cheatham. There the struggle was hard, and there it lasted longest. From the fact that I had seen no infantry in my front, and heard no musketry near, I thought I was exempted from the general infantry attack. I was therefore surprised and awakened from my dream when a courier came to me, about 9 o'clock, and said that Gen. Ector was at once directed to send two regiments to report to him. Soon after a second courier came and reported an assault made on the left of my line. I went immediately with the remainder of Ector's Brigade to Cockrell's assistance, but on reaching him I found the Federal assault had been repulsed. The assaulting column had struck Cockrell's works near the center, recoiled under the fire, swung around into a steep valley where, exposed to the direct fire of the Missourians in front and right and of Sears's Mississippians on their left, it seemed to melt away, or sink into the earth, to rise no more.[24]

Appendix I

Report of Brig. Gen. Morgan L. Smith, USA, Commanding Second Division, Fifteenth Corps, Army of the Tennessee

I have the honor to submit the following report of an assault made by a part of General Logan's corps, under my command, upon the enemy's works to the right of Kenesaw Mountain:

In accordance with General Logan's order, I withdrew my division from its position to the left of the mountain after dark on the night of the 26th instant, and massed it opposite the extreme right of the mountain and a hill, which is a continuation of the same, to the right. This [Pigeon] hill was the objective point of the assault, and my division and Colonel Walcutt's brigade, of General Harrow's division, was designated as the assaulting column, and 8 a.m. of the 27th the hour to advance. General Lightburn, commanding Second Brigade, of about 2,000 muskets, was directed to form in two lines and assault through a little orchard, about 400 yards to the right of the hill, and to advance as soon as he heard a brisk fire on the left. General Giles A. Smith, commanding First Brigade, of about the same strength, was directed to move at the same time in two lines directly on the hill. Colonel Walcutt, commanding the brigade of General Harrow's division, of about 1,500 muskets, was directed to

Pigeon Hill, Kennesaw Mountain National Battlefield Park. Photo by the author.

move directly for the gorge where the hill joins on to the mountain, lapping the mountain and left of the hill, feel into the gorge as far as possible, and capture the works in his front. As the enemy could not depress their artillery sufficiently to fire on him, he was ordered to advance first, and the opening of the enemy's fire upon him was the signal for the other two brigades to advance. The line moved about 8 o'clock. It advanced steadily, with a strong line of skirmishers, but owing to the extreme density of the underbrush it was impossible for skirmishers to keep in front of their lines. Found the enemy's line of rifle-pits about 400 yards from their main works, and killed or captured most of their skirmishers. After passing a deep, swampy ravine, the line fixed bayonets, advancing, moved steadily and rapidly for the enemy's works, amidst a shower of shot and shell. Officers and men fell thick and fast. In addition to the steepness of the ascent, trees had been felled and brush and rocks piled in such a manner as to make it impossible to advance with any regularity. Officers and men still pushed forward. Reenforcements [sic] of the enemy were seen coming in from the right and left. Within about thirty feet of the enemy's main works the line staggered and sought cover as best they could behind logs and rocks. Some of the Fifty-fifth and One hundred and eleventh Illinois, of General Giles A. Smith's brigade, fell on and inside the works. General Lightburn, on the right, pressed on through a swamp, where officers and men sank to their knees, and a very dense thicket, but on account of an enfilading fire, was unable to get nearer than 150 yards of the orchard and works beyond. He, however, by coming suddenly out of the thicket and swamp, killed and wounded quite a number of the enemy and captured 2 officers and 36 men.

Colonel Barnhill, commanding Fortieth Illinois, of Colonel Walcutt's brigade, and (Captain) Augustin, Fifty-fifth Illinois, were killed on the hill near the enemy's works; Colonel Rice, Fifty-seventh Ohio, also wounded on the hill (leg amputated); Colonel Spooner, Eighty-third Indiana, farther to the right of the hill, was wounded (arm amputated at the shoulder); Colonel Parry, Forty-seventh Ohio, severely in the leg.

Colonel Walcutt, commanding the brigade from General Harrow's division, moved forward promptly toward the gorge, encountered the enemy's rifle-pits; captured about 50 prisoners; found the gorge perfectly impassable on account of the rocky and precipitous

Appendix I

> entrance. He then turned his attention to the right of the mountain, from which he was receiving a flank fire, and left of the hill; some of his brigade met their fate at the breast-works. Officers and men on the side-hill were completely covered by the second line and sharpshooters, and the artillery of Generals Osterhaus' and Harrow's divisions, so that I am satisfied not one prisoner was taken by the enemy. A good line of rifle-pits was made in front of General G. A. Smith's and Colonel Walcutt's brigades in one hour, within 100 yards of the hill in some places. At dark the men were all withdrawn from side-hill; our pickets were relieved by General Osterhaus, and I received General Logan's order to resume the position occupied in the morning.[25]

The final two tour stops are two cemeteries: the Marietta Confederate Cemetery and the (Union) Marietta National Cemetery, both located in the city's downtown. The first destination, Stop 8, is the Confederate Cemetery. Leave the parking lot, and retrace your drive 1.2 miles east and southeast on Burnt Hickory Road NW to the intersection with Whitlock Avenue NW (GA 120). Turn left (east), and proceed 1.4 miles to the intersection with South Marietta Parkway SE / GA 120 / GA 360 / GA 5. Turn right (south) onto South Marietta Parkway SE. Continue 0.4 mile, curve left (east), and merge into the right lane, passing under the railroad bridge. At the intersection with Atlanta Street /GA 5, turn right (southeast). Continue on about 0.4 mile, paralleling the railroad tracks on your right (southwest). Take the first available right (southwest) turn, East Dixie Avenue / GA 5, turn right (southwest), cross the railroad tracks, and turn right again (northwest) on West Atlanta Street. Continue northwest on West Atlanta Street, paralleling the railroad tracks now on your right (northeast). Pass through the intersections with Gramling Street SE, West Dixie Avenue SE, Hedges Street SE, and Cemetery Street SE. At the second entrance to the cemetery on your left, indicated by a sign, turn left. Drive northwest to the top of the hill, which is in the midst of the Confederate section of the cemetery. If you arrive at the entrance to Brown Park, you have driven too far. Park safely, and explore the cemetery as desired.

Stop 8: Marietta Confederate Cemetery

Critical Decisions: (9) Sherman Orders an Assault on the Center of the Kennesaw Mountain Line, (11) Sherman Outflanks Johnston to Advance toward the Chattahoochee River

Driving Tour of the Critical Decisions of the Battle of Kennesaw Mountain

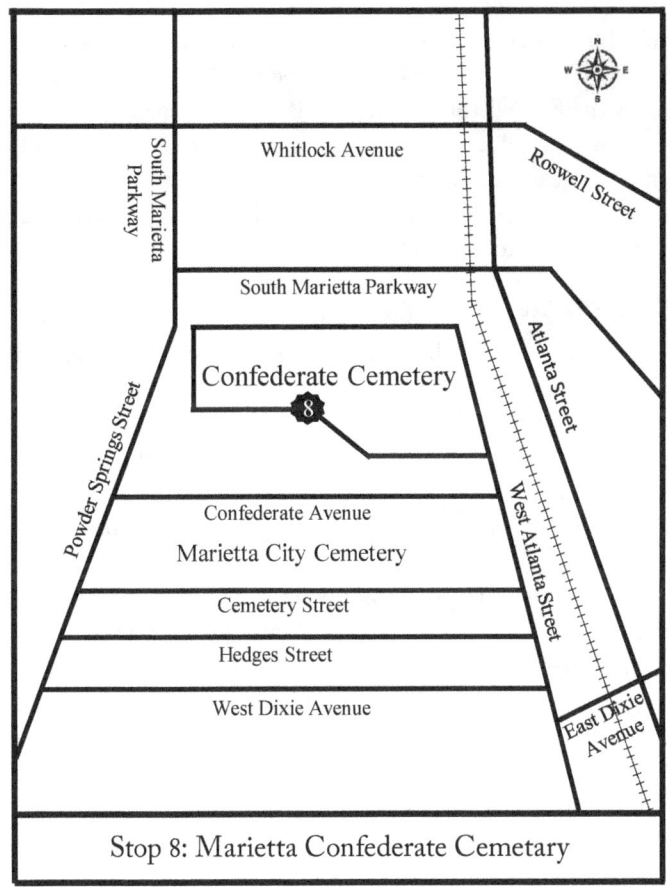

Stop 8: Marietta Confederate Cemetary

Narrative of Gen. Joseph E. Johnston, CSA, Commanding Department and Army of Tennessee

On the 29th a truce was agreed to, to permit the Federal soldiers to bury their dead lying near our breastworks [along the Kennesaw Mountain Line].

The reports from the flanks showed that the enemy had much reduced the cavalry of their left, and proportionally increased the strength of that of their right. Major-General [Gustavus W.] Smith [First Division, Georgia Militia] was therefore desired to bring

Appendix I

forward his division to the support of Jackson's troops. It was done; and the State troops under him rendered good service.

As the Federal commander manifested a strong disposition to operate by his right, which was already nearer to Atlanta than the Confederate left, another position was selected for the army, ten miles south of Marietta, which Colonel Prestman [*sic*]was desired to have prepared for occupation; and Brigadier-General Shoupe was directed to construct a line of redoubts [Shoupades] on a plan devised by himself, on a line selected by Major-General Lovell on the high ground near the Chattahoochee, and covering the approaches to the railroad bridge and Turner's Ferry. Negro laborers had been impressed for the work. Some time before, Captain Grant, the engineer-officer who directed the construction of the intrenchments around Atlanta, was instructed to strengthen them in a manner explained to him, and was authorized to impress negro laborers for the work.

The reports of outposts, and observation from the top of Kenesaw [*sic*] on the 1st and 2d of July, showed that General Sherman was transferring strong bodies of troops to his right. The Confederate army was therefore moved to the position prepared for it by Colonel Prestman[*sic*], which it reached early on the 3d, and occupied two lines crossing the road to Atlanta almost at right angles—Loring's corps on the right and Hardee's on the left of the road, Hood's on

Marietta Confederate Cemetery, Marietta, GA. Photo by the author.

Driving Tour of the Critical Decisions of the Battle of Kennesaw Mountain

> the left of Hardee's, Wheeler's on the fight of Loring's corps and Jackson's, supported by General Smith, on the left of Hood's [the Smyrna Line].[26]

The final stop is the (Union) Marietta National Cemetery. Depart the cemetery by returning to West Atlanta Street. Turn right (southeast) onto West Atlanta Street, and follow it southeast back to the intersection with East Dixie Avenue / GA 5. Turn left (northeast), cross the railroad tracks, and turn left (northwest) back onto Atlanta Street SE. Continue north, crossing South Marietta Parkway SE. Continue north three blocks to the intersection with Roswell Street NE. Turn right (east) onto Roswell Street NE, and continue one block east past Waddell Street NE. After crossing Waddell Street NE, as the street turns southeast, take the next left turn (northeast) onto Haynes Street NE, followed by an immediate right turn (east) onto Washington Street NE. Drive two blocks to the entrance to the National Cemetery on the southeast corner of the intersection of Cole Street NE and Washington Street NE. Park, and explore the cemetery as desired.

Stop 9: Marietta National Cemetery

Critical Decisions: (9) Sherman Orders an Assault on the Center of the Kennesaw Mountain Line, (11) Sherman Outflanks Johnston to Advance Toward the Chattahoochee River

Marietta National Cemetery, Marietta, GA.
Photo by the author.

Appendix I

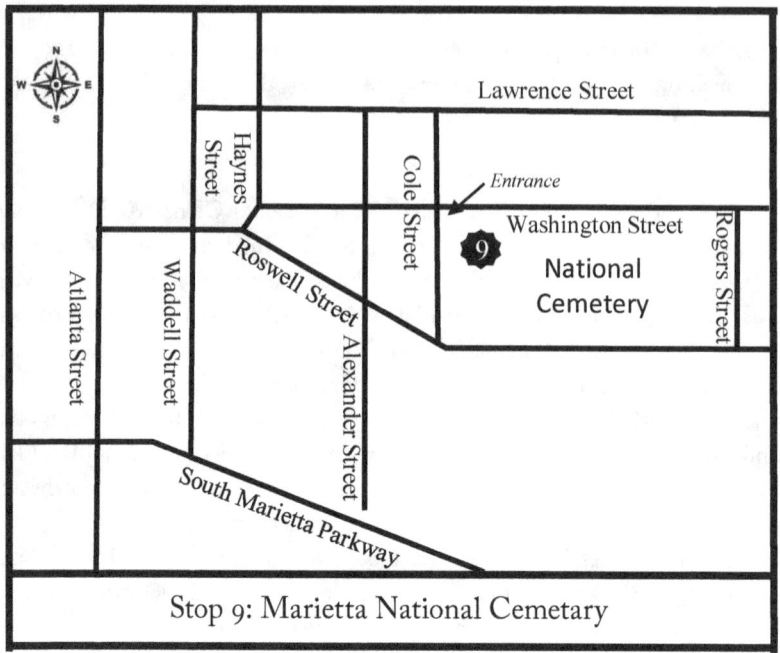

Stop 9: Marietta National Cemetary

Narrative of Maj. Gen. William T. Sherman, USA, Commanding Military Division of the Mississippi

While the battle was in progress at the centre, Schofield crossed Olley's Creek on the right and gained a position threatening Johnston's line of retreat; and, to increase the effect, I ordered Stoneman's cavalry to proceed rapidly still farther to the right, to Sweetwater. Satisfied of the bloody cost of attacking intrenched lines, I at once thought of moving the whole army to the railroad at a point (Fulton) about ten miles below Marietta, or to the Chattahoochee River itself, a movement similar to the one afterward so successfully practiced at Atlanta. All the orders were issued to bring forward supplies enough to fill our wagons, intending to strip the railroad back to Allatoona, and leave that place as our depot, to be covered as well as possible by Garrard's cavalry. General Thomas, as usual, shook his head, deeming it risky to leave the railroad; but something had to be done. . . .

> McPherson drew out of his lines during the night of July 2d, leaving Garrard's cavalry, dismounted, occupying his trenches, and moved to the rear of the Army of the Cumberland, stretching down the Nickajack; but Johnston detected the movement, and promptly abandoned Marietta and Kenesaw [sic]. I expected as much, for, by the earliest dawn of the 3d of July, I was up at a large spy-glass mounted on a tripod, which Colonel Poe, United States Engineers, had at his bivouac close by our camp. I directed the glass on Kenesaw [sic], and saw some of our pickets crawling up the hill cautiously; soon they stood upon the very top, and I could plainly see their movements as they ran along the crest just abandoned by the enemy. In a moment I roused my staff, and started them off with orders in every direction for a pursuit by every possible road, hoping to catch Johnston in the confusion of retreat, especially at the crossing of the Chattahoochee River.[27]

Unfortunately, here lie the remains of at least some of Sherman's soldiers who paid the ultimate price for his fighting at and around the Kennesaw Mountain Line.

This concludes the driving tour of the critical decisions of the Battle of Kennesaw Mountain. You can reach I-75, going either north or south, by leaving the cemetery, turning right (north), crossing Washington Street NE, and driving north on Cole Street NE six blocks to the intersection with North Marietta Parkway / GA 120. Turn right (east) onto North Marietta Parkway, and proceed about 1.5 miles to the entrance ramps to I-75, or depart elsewhere at your discretion.

APPENDIX II

UNION ORDER OF BATTLE

BATTLE OF KOLB'S FARM
June 22, 1864

ARMY OF THE CUMBERLAND
Maj. Gen. George H. Thomas

TWENTIETH ARMY CORPS
Maj. Gen. Joseph Hooker

ESCORT
Company K, 15th Illinois Cavalry, Capt. William Duncan

FIRST DIVISION
Brig. Gen. Alpheus S. Williams

FIRST BRIGADE
Brig Gen. Joseph F. Knipe
5th Connecticut, Col. Warren W. Packer
3rd Maryland Detachment, Lieut. Col. David Gove
123rd New York, Lieut. Col. James C. Rogers
141st New York, Col. William K. Logie
46th Pennsylvania, Col. James L. Selfridge

Second Brigade
Brig. Gen. Thomas H. Ruger
27th Indiana, Col. Silas Colgrove
2nd Massachusetts, Col. William Cogswell
13th New Jersey, Col. Ezra A. Carman
107th New York, Col. Nirom M. Crane
150th New York, Col. John H. Ketcham
3rd Wisconsin, Col. William Hawley

Third Brigade
Col. James S. Robinson
82nd Illinois, Lieut. Col. Edward S. Salomon
101st Illinois, Lieut. Col. John B. Le Sage
45th New York, Col. Adolphus Dobke
143rd New York, Col. Horace Broughton
61st Ohio, Col. Stephen J. McGroarty
82nd Ohio, Col. David Thompson

Artillery
Capt. John D. Woodbury
1st New York Light Battery I, Lieut. Charles E. Winegar
1st New York Light Battery M, Capt. John D. Woodbury

SECOND DIVISION
Brig. Gen. John W. Geary

First Brigade
Col. Charles Candy
5th Ohio, Lieut. Col. R. L. Kilpatrick
29th Ohio, Capt. Myron T. Wright
66th Ohio, Lieut. Col. Eugene Powell
28th Pennsylvania, Lieut. Col. John Flynn
147th Pennsylvania, Col. Ario Pardee

Second Brigade
Col. Patrick H. Jones
33rd New Jersey, Col. George W. Mindil
119th New York, Capt. Charles H. Odell
134th New York, Lieut. Col. Allan H. Jackson
154th New York, Maj. Lewis D. Warner
73rd Pennsylvania, Maj. Charles C. Cresson
109th Pennsylvania, Capt. Walter G. Dunn

THIRD BRIGADE
    Col. David Ireland
    60th New York, Col. Abel Godard
    78th New York, Lieut. Col. Harvey S. Chatsfield
    102nd New York, Col. Herbert von Hammerstein
    137th New York, Lieut. Col. Koert S. Van Voohis
    149th New York, Col. Henry A. Barnum
    29th Pennsylvania, Maj. Jesse R. Millison
    111th Pennsylvania, Col. George A. Cobham Jr.

ARTILLERY
    Capt. William Wheeler
    Capt. Charles C. Aleshire
    13th New York Light Battery, Capt. William Wheeler,
        Lieut. Henry Bundy
    Pennsylvania Light Battery E, Capt. James D. McGill

ARMY OF THE OHIO (TWENTY-THIRD CORPS)
    Maj. Gen. John M. Schofield

SECOND DIVISION
    Brig. Gen. Milo S. Hascall

THIRD BRIGADE
    Col. Silas A. Strickland
    14th Kentucky, Col. George W. Gallup
    20th Kentucky, Lieut. Col. Thomas B. Waller
    27th Kentucky, Lieut. Col. John H. Ward
    50th Ohio, Lieut. Col. George R. Elstner

BATTLE OF KENNESAW MOUNTAIN
June 27, 1864

MILITARY DIVISION OF THE MISSISSIPPI
    Maj. Gen. William T. Sherman

CHIEF OF ARTILLERY
    Brig. Gen. William F. Barry

CHIEF OF ORDANCE
    Capt. Thomas G. Taylor

CHIEF OF ENGINEERS
Capt. Orlando M. Poe

MEDICAL DIRECTOR
Lieut. Col. Edward D. Kittoe

HEADQUARTERS GUARD
7th Company, Ohio Sharpshooters, Lieut. William McCrory

ARMY OF THE CUMBERLAND
Maj. Gen. George H. Thomas

CHIEF OF ARTILLERY
Brig. Gen. John M. Brannan

CHIEF OF ORDNANCE
Lieut. Otho E. Michaelis

CHIEF ENGINEER
Lieut. Henry C. Wharton

MEDICAL DIRECTOR
Surg. George E. Cooper

ESCORT
Company I, 1st Ohio Cavalry, Lieut. Henry C. Reppert

FOURTH ARMY CORPS
Maj. Gen. Oliver O. O. Howard

CHIEF OF ARTILLERY
Capt. Lyman Bridges

FIRST DIVISION
Maj. Gen. David S. Stanley

First Brigade
Col. Isaac M. Kirby
21st Illinois, Maj. James E. Calloway
38th Illinois, Col. William T. Chapman
31st Indiana, Col. John T. Smith

81st Indiana, Lieut. Col. William C. Wheeler
1st Kentucky, Col. David A. Enyart
2nd Kentucky, Lieut. Col. John R. Hurd
90th Ohio, Lieut. Col. Samuel N. Yeoman
101st Ohio, Col. Isaac M. Kirby

SECOND BRIGADE
Brig. Gen. Walter C. Whitaker
96th Illinois, Col. Thomas E. Champion
115th Illinois, Col. Jessie H. Moore
35th Indiana, Maj. John P. Dufficy
84th Indiana, Col. Andrew J. Neff
21st Kentucky, Col. Samuel W. Price
40th Ohio, Col. Jacob B. Taylor
45th Ohio, Lieut. Col. Charles H. Butterfield
51st Ohio, Lieut. Col. Charles H. Wood

THIRD BRIGADE
Col. William Grose
59th Illinois, Col. P. Sidney Post
75th Illinois, Col. John E. Bennett
80th Illinois, Lieut. Col. William M. Kilgour
84th Illinois, Col. Louis H. Waters
9th Indiana, Col. Isaac C. B. Suman
30th Indiana, Lieut. Col. Orrin D. Hurd
36th Indiana, Lieut. Col. Oliver H. P. Carey
77th Pennsylvania, Col. Thomas E. Rose

ARTILLERY
Capt. Samuel M. McDowell
Capt. Theodore S. Thomasson
5th Indiana Light Battery, Capt. Alfred Morrison
Pennsylvania Light Battery B, Capt. Jacob Ziegler

SECOND DIVISION
Brig. Gen. John Newton

FIRST BRIGADE
Brig. Gen. Nathan Kimball
36th Illinois, Col. Silas Miller, Capt. James B. McNeal
44th Illinois, Col. Wallace W. Barrett
73rd Illinois, Maj. Thomas W. Motherspaw
74th Illinois, Lieut. Col. James B. Kerr, Capt. Thomas J. Bryan

Appendix II

    88th Illinois, Lieut. Col. George W. Chandler,
        Lieut. Col. George W. Smith
    15th Missouri, Col. Joseph Conrad
    24th Wisconsin, Maj. Arthur MacArthur Jr.

SECOND BRIGADE
    Brig. Gen. George D. Wagner
    100th Illinois, Maj. Charles W. Hammond
    40th Indiana, Col. John W. Blake
    57th Indiana, Lieut. Col. Willis Blanch
    28th Kentucky, Col. J. Rowan Boone, Maj. George W. Barth
    26th Ohio, Maj. Norris T. Peatman, Capt. Lewis D. Adair
    97th Ohio, Col. John Q. Lane

THIRD BRIGADE
    Brig. Gen. Charles G. Harker
    Brig. Gen. Luther P. Bradley
    27th Illinois, Lieut. Col. William A. Schmitt
    42nd Illinois, Capt. Jared W. Richards
    51st Illinois, Col. Luther P. Bradley
    79th Illinois, Lieut. Col. Henry E. Rives
    3rd Kentucky, Col. Henry C. Dunlap
    64th Ohio, Maj. Samuel L. Coulter
    65th Ohio, Lieut. Col. Horatio N. Whitbeck, Capt. Charles O. Tannehill
    125th Ohio, Lieut. Col. David H. Moore

ARTILLERY
    Capt. Wilbur F. Goodspeed
    1st Illinois Light Battery M, Capt. George W. Spencer
    1st Ohio Light Battery A, Lieut. Charles W. Scovill

THIRD DIVISION
    Brig. Gen. Thomas J. Wood

FIRST BRIGADE
    Col. Richard H. Nodine
    25th Illinois, Lieut. Col. Westford Taggert
    35th Illinois, Lieut. Col. William P. Chandler
    89th Illinois, Col. Charles T. Hotchkiss
    32nd Indiana, Col. Frank Erdelmeyer
    8th Kansas, Col. John A. Martin
    15th Ohio, Col. William Wallace

49th Ohio, Lieut. Col. Samuel F. Gray
15th Wisconsin, Maj. George Wilson

SECOND BRIGADE
Brig. Gen. William B. Hazen
6th Indiana, Lieut. Col. Calvin D. Campbell
5th Kentucky, Col. William W. Berry
6th Kentucky, Maj. Richard T. Whitaker
23rd Kentucky, Lieut. Col. James C. Foy
41st Ohio, Lieut. Col. Robert L. Kimberly
71st Ohio, Col. Henry K. McConnell
93rd Ohio, Lieut. Col. Daniel Bowman
124th Ohio, Col. Oliver H. Payne

THIRD BRIGADE
Col. Frederick Knefler
79th Indiana, Col. Frederick Knefler
86th Indiana, Col. George F. Dick
9th Kentucky, Col. George H. Cram
17th Kentucky, Col. Alexander M. Stout
13th Ohio, Col. Dwight Jarvis
19th Ohio, Col. Charles F. Manderson
59th Ohio, Capt. R. H. Higgens

ARTILLERY
Lieut. Lyman A. White
Bridges Illinois Light Battery, Lieut. Lyman A. White
6th Ohio Light Battery, Lieut. Oliver H. P. Ayres

FOURTEENTH ARMY CORPS
Maj. Gen. John M. Palmer

FIRST DIVISION
Brig. Gen. John H. King

PROVOST GUARD
Capt. Charles F. Trowbridge
Company D, 1st Battalion, 16th United States Regiment

FIRST BRIGADE
Brig. Gen. William P. Carlin
104th Illinois, Lieut. Col. Douglas Hapeman

Appendix II

42nd Indiana, Lieut. Col. William T. B. McIntire
88th Indiana, Lieut. Col. Cyrus E. Briant
15th Kentucky, Col. Marion C. Taylor
2nd Ohio, Col. Anson G. McCook
33rd Ohio, Lieut. Col. James H. M. Montgomery
94th Ohio, Col. Rue P. Hutchins
10th Wisconsin, Capt. Jacob W. Roby
21st Wisconsin, Lieut. Col. Harrison C. Hobart

SECOND BRIGADE
Col. William L. Stoughton
11th Michigan, Lieut. Col. Melvin B. Mudge
15th US (6 companies), Maj. John R. Edie
15th US (9 companies), Capt. A. B. Dod
16th US. (4 companies), Capt. Robert P. Barry
16th US (4 companies), Capt. Alexander H. Stanton
18th US (8 companies), Capt. George W. Smith
18th US (4 companies), Capt. William J. Fetterman
19th US (5 companies), Capt. James Mooney

THIRD BRIGADE
Col. Benjamin Scribner
37th Indiana, Lieut. Col. William D. Ward
38th Indiana, Lieut. Col. Daniel F. Griffin
21st Ohio, Lieut. Col. Arnold McMahon
74th Ohio, Col. Josiah Given
78th Pennsylvania, Col. William Sirwell
79th Pennsylvania, Maj. Michael H. Locher
1st Wisconsin, Lieut. Col. George B. Bingham

ARTILLERY
Capt. Lucius H. Drury
1st Illinois Light Battery C, Capt. Mark H. Prescott
1st Ohio Battery I, Capt. Hubert Dilger

SECOND DIVISION
Brig. Gen. Jefferson C. Davis

FIRST BRIGADE
Brig. Gen. James D. Morgan
10th Illinois, Col. John Tillson
16th Illinois, Col. Robert F. Smith
60th Illinois, Col. William B. Anderson

10th Michigan, Col. Charles M. Lum
14th Michigan, Col. Henry R. Mizner

SECOND BRIGADE
Col. John G. Mitchell
34th Illinois, Lieut. Col. Oscar Van Tassell
78th Illinois, Col. Carter Van Vleck
98th Ohio, Lieut. Col. John S. Pearce
113th Ohio, Lieut. Col. Darius B. Warner, Maj. Lyne S. Sullivant
121st Ohio, Col. Henry B. Banning

THIRD BRIGADE
Col. Daniel McCook
Col. Oscar F. Harmon
Col. Caleb J. Dilworth
85th Illinois, Col. Caleb J. Dilworth, Maj. Robert G. Rider
86th Illinois, Lieut. Col. Allen L. Fahnestack
125th Illinois, Col. Oscar F. Harmon, Maj. John B. Lee
22nd Indiana, Capt. William H. Snodgrass
52nd Ohio, Lieut. Col. Charles W. Clancy

ARTILLERY
Capt. Charles M. Barnett
2nd Illinois Light Battery I, Lieut. Alonzo W. Coe
5th Wisconsin Light Battery and 2nd Minnesota Battery (detachment), Capt. George Q. Gardner

THIRD DIVISION
Brig. Gen. Absalom Baird

FIRST BRIGADE
Brig. Gen. John B. Turchin
24th Illinois, Capt. August Mauff
82nd Indiana, Col. Morton C. Hunter
23rd Missouri, Col. William P. Robinson
17th Ohio, Col. Durbin Ward
31st Ohio, Col. Moses B. Walker
89th Ohio, Col. Caleb H. Carlton
92nd Ohio, Col. Benjamin D. Fearing

SECOND BRIGADE
Col. Newell Gleason
75th Indiana, Col. William O'Brien
87th Indiana, Lieut. Col. Edwin P. Hammond

101st Indiana, Lieut. Col. Thomas Doan
2nd Minnesota, Col. James George
35th Ohio, Maj. Joseph L. Budd
105th Ohio, Lieut. Col. George T. Perkins

THIRD BRIGADE
Col. George P. Este
10th Indiana, Lieut. Col. Marsh B. Taylor
74th Indiana, Lieut. Col. Myron Baker
10th Kentucky, Col. William H. Hays
14th Ohio, Maj. John W. Wilson
38th Ohio, Col. William A. Choate

ARTILLERY
Capt. George Estep
7th Indiana Light Battery, Capt. Otho H. Morgan
19th Indiana Light Battery, Lieut. William P. Stackhouse

TWENTIETH ARMY CORPS
Maj. Gen. Joseph Hooker

ESCORT
Company K, 15th Illinois Cavalry, Capt. William Duncan

FIRST DIVISION
Brig. Gen. Alpheus S. Williams

FIRST BRIGADE
Brig Gen. Joseph F. Knipe
5th Connecticut, Col. Warren W. Packer
3rd Maryland Detachment, Lieut. Col. David Gove
123rd New York, Lieut. Col. James C. Rogers
141st New York, Col. William K. Logie
46th Pennsylvania, Col. James L. Selfridge

SECOND BRIGADE
Brig. Gen. Thomas H. Ruger
27th Indiana, Col. Silas Colgrove
2nd Massachusetts, Col. William Cogswell
13th New Jersey, Col. Ezra A. Carman
107th New York, Col. Nirom M. Crane
150th New York, Col. John H. Ketcham
3rd Wisconsin, Col. William Hawley

Third Brigade
Col. James S. Robinson
82nd Illinois, Lieut. Col. Edward S. Salomon
101st Illinois, Lieut. Col. John B. Le Sage
45th New York, Col. Adolphus Dobke
143rd New York, Col. Horace Broughton
61st Ohio, Col. Stephen J. McGroarty
82nd Ohio, Col. David Thompson

Artillery
Capt. John D. Woodbury
1st New York Light Battery I, Lieut. Charles E. Winegar
1st New York Light Battery M, Capt. John D. Woodbury

SECOND DIVISION
Brig. Gen. John W. Geary

First Brigade
Col. Charles Candy
5th Ohio, Lieut. Col. R. L. Kilpatrick
29th Ohio, Capt. Myron T. Wright
66th Ohio, Lieut. Col. Eugene Powell
28th Pennsylvania, Lieut. Col. John Flynn
147th Pennsylvania, Col. Ario Pardee

Second Brigade
Col. Patrick H. Jones
33rd New Jersey, Col. George W. Mindil
119th New York, Capt. Charles H. Odell
134th New York, Lieut. Col. Allan H. Jackson
154th New York, Maj. Lewis D. Warner
73rd Pennsylvania, Maj. Charles C. Cresson
109th Pennsylvania, Capt. Walter G. Dunn

Third Brigade
Col. David Ireland
60th New York, Col. Abel Godard
78th New York, Lieut. Col. Harvey S. Chatsfield
102nd New York, Col. Herbert von Hammerstein
137th New York, Lieut. Col. Koert S. Van Voohis
149th New York, Col. Henry A. Barnum
29th Pennsylvania, Maj. Jesse R. Millison
111th Pennsylvania, Col. George A. Cobham Jr.

ARTILLERY
  Capt. Charles C. Aleshire
  13th New York Light Battery, Capt. William Wheeler,
    Lieut. Henry Bundy
  Pennsylvania Light Battery E, Capt. James D. McGill

THIRD DIVISION
Maj. Gen. Daniel Butterfield

FIRST BRIGADE
  Col. Benjamin Harrison
  102nd Illinois, Col. Franklin C. Smith
  105th Illinois, Col. Daniel Dustin
  129th Illinois, Col. Henry Chase
  70th Indiana, Lieut. Col. Samuel Merrill
  79th Ohio, Col. Henry G. Kennett

SECOND BRIGADE
  Col. John Coburn
  33rd Indiana, Maj. Levin T. Miller
  85th Indiana, Col. John P. Baird
  19th Michigan, Maj. Eli A. Griffin
  22nd Wisconsin, Col. William L. Utley

THIRD BRIGADE
  Col. James Wood
  20th Connecticut, Col. Samuel Ross
  33rd Massachusetts, Lieut. Col. Godfrey Rider
  136th New York, Lieut. Col. Lester B. Faulkner
  55th Ohio, Lieut. Col. Edwin H. Powers
  73rd Ohio, Maj. Samuel H. Hurst
  26th Wisconsin, Lieut. Col. Frederick C. Winkler

ARTILLERY
  Capt. Marco B. Gary
  1st Michigan Light Battery I, Capt. Luther R. Smith
  1st Ohio Light Battery C, Lieut. Jerome B. Stephens

RESERVE BRIGADE
  Col. Heber Le Favour
  9th Michigan, Lieut. Col. William Wilkinson
  22nd Michigan, Lieut. Col. Henry S. Dean

PONTONIERS
    Col. George P. Buell
    58th Indiana, Lieut. Col. Joseph Moore
AMMUNITION TRAIN GUARD
    1st Battalion Ohio Sharpshooters, Capt. Gershom M. Barber
SIEGE ARTILLERY
    11th Indiana Battery, Capt. Arnold Sutermeister

ARMY OF THE TENNESSEE
Maj. Gen. James B. McPherson

CHIEF OF ARTILLERY
Capt. Andrew Hickenlooper

CHIEF ENGINEER
Capt. Chauncey B. Reese

MEDICAL DIRECTOR
Surg. John Moore

ESCORT
4th Company Ohio Cavalry, Capt. John S. Foster
Company B, 1st Ohio Cavalry, Capt. George F. Conn

FIFTEENTH ARMY CORPS
Maj. Gen. John A. Logan

FIRST DIVISION
Brig. Gen. Peter J. Osterhaus

FIRST BRIGADE
    Brig. Gen. Charles R. Woods
    26th Iowa, Col. Milo Smith
    30th Iowa, Lieut. Col. Aurelius Roberts
    27th Missouri, Col. Thomas Curly
    76th Ohio, Col. William B. Woods
SECOND BRIGADE
    Col. James A. Williamson
    4th Iowa, Lieut. Col. Samuel D. Nichols

9th Iowa, Col. David Carskaddon
25th Iowa, Col. George A. Stone
31st Iowa, Col. William Smyth

THIRD BRIGADE
Col. Hugo Wangelin
3rd Missouri, Col. Theodore Meumann
12th Missouri, Lieut. Col. Jacob Kaercher
17th Missouri, Maj. Francis Romer
29th Missouri, Lieut. Col. Joseph S. Gage
31st Missouri, Lieut. Col. Samuel P. Simpson
32nd Missouri, Maj. Abraham J. Seay

ARTILLERY
Maj. Clemens Landgraeber
2nd Missouri Light Battery F, Capt. Louis Voelkner
4th Ohio Light Battery, Capt. George Froehlich

SECOND DIVISION
Brig. Gen. Morgan L. Smith

FIRST BRIGADE
Brig. Gen. Giles A. Smith
55th Illinois, Lieut. Col. Theodore C. Chandler
111th Illinois, Col. James S. Martin
116th Illinois, Capt. John S. Windsor
127th Illinois, Capt. Alexander C. Little
6th Missouri, Lieut. Col. Delos Van Deusen
8th Missouri, (only Company K), Lieut. Col. David C. Coleman
57th Ohio, Col. Americus V. Rice, Lieut. Col. Samuel R. Mott

SECOND BRIGADE
Brig. Gen. Joseph Lightburn
83rd Indiana, Col. Benjamin J. Spooner, Capt. George H. Scott
30th Ohio, Col. Theodore Jones
37th Ohio, Maj. Charles Hipp
47th Ohio, Col. Augustus C. Perry, Lieut. Col. John Wallace
53rd Ohio, Col. Wells S. Jones
54th Ohio, Lieut. Col. Robert Williams Jr.

ARTILLERY
Capt. Francis De Gress
1st Illinois Light Battery A, Lieut. George McCagg Jr.

1st Illinois Light Battery B, Capt. Israel P. Rumsey
1st Illinois Light Battery H, Capt. Francis De Gress

THIRD DIVISION
Brig. Gen. John E. Smith
Deployed guarding the railroad, headquarters at Cartersville

FOURTH DIVISION
Brig. Gen. William Harrow

FIRST BRIGADE
Col. Reuben Williams
26th Illinois, Lieut. Col. Robert A. Gillmore
90th Illinois, Lieut. Col. Owen Stuart
12th Indiana, Lieut. Col. James Goodnow
100th Indiana, Lieut. Col. Albert Heath
15th Michigan, Lieut. Col. Frederick S. Hutchinson
70th Ohio, Capt. Louis Love

SECOND BRIGADE
Brig. Gen. Charles C. Walcutt
40th Illinois, Lieut. Col. Rigdon S. Barnhill, Maj. Hiram W. Hall
103rd Illinois, Lieut. Col. George W. Wright, Capt. Franklin C. Post
97th Indiana, Lieut. Col. Aden G. Cavins
6th Iowa, Maj. Thomas J. Ennis
46th Ohio, Capt. Joshua W. Heath

THIRD BRIGADE
Col. John M. Oliver
48th Illinois, Col. Lucien Greathouse
99th Indiana, Col. Alexander Fowler
15th Michigan, Lieut. Col. Frederick S. Hutchinson
70th Ohio, Maj. William B. Brown

ARTILLERY
Maj. John T. Cheney
1st Illinois Light Battery F, Capt. Josiah H. Burton
1st Iowa Light Battery, Capt. Henry Griffiths

SIXTEENTH ARMY CORPS
Maj. Gen. Grenville M. Dodge

ESCORT
    1st Alabama Cavalry, Col. George L. Godfrey
    Company A, 52nd Illinois, Capt. George E. Young

SECOND DIVISION
    Brig. Gen. Thomas W. Sweeny

FIRST BRIGADE
    Brig. Gen. Elliott W. Rice
    52nd Illinois, Lieut. Col. Edwin A. Bowen
    66th Indiana, Lieut. Col. Roger Martin
    2nd Iowa, Lieut. Col. Noel B. Howard
    7th Iowa, Lieut. Col. James C. Parrott

SECOND BRIGADE
    Col. August Mersy
    9th Illinois Mounted Infantry, Maj. John H. Kuhn
    12th Illinois, Lieut. Col. Henry Van Sellar
    66th Illinois, Capt. William S. Boyd
    8th Ohio, Lieut. Col. Robert N. Adams

THIRD BRIGADE
    Stationed at Rome, Georgia

ARTILLERY
    Capt. Frederick Welker
    1st Missouri Light Battery H, Lieut. Andrew T. Blodgett

FOURTH DIVISION
    Brig. Gen. James C. Veatch

FIRST BRIGADE
    Brig. Gen. John W. Fuller
    64th Illinois, Col. John Morrill
    18th Missouri, Lieut. Col. Charles S. Sheldon
    27th Ohio, Lieut. Col. Mendal Churchill
    39th Ohio, Col. Edward F. Noyes

SECOND BRIGADE
    Brig. Gen. John W. Sprague
    35th New Jersey, Col. John J. Cladek
    43rd Ohio, Col. Wager Swayne

63rd Ohio, Lieut. Col. Charles E. Brown
25th Wisconsin, Col. Milton Montgomery

THIRD BRIGADE
Stationed at Decatur, Alabama

ARTILLERY
Capt. Jerome B. Burrows
1st Michigan Light Battery C, Capt. George Robinson
14th Ohio Light Battery, Capt. Jerome B. Burrows
2nd United States Battery F, Capt. Albert M. Murry

SEVENTEENTH ARMY CORPS
Maj. Gen. Francis P. Blair

ESCORT
Company G, 9th Illinois Mounted Infantry, Capt. Isaac Clements

THIRD DIVISION
Brig. Gen. Mortimer D. Leggett

ESCORT
Company D, 1st Ohio Cavalry, Lieut. James W. Kirkendall

FIRST BRIGADE
Brig. Gen. Manning F. Force
20th Illinois, Lieut. Col. Daniel Bradley
30th Illinois, Col. Warren Shedd
31st Illinois, Lieut. Col. Robert N. Pearson
16th Wisconsin, Col. Cassius Fairchild

SECOND BRIGADE
Col. Robert K. Scott
20th Ohio, Lieut. Col. John C. Fry
32nd Ohio, Col. Benjamin F. Potts
68th Ohio, Lieut. Col. George E. Wells
78th Ohio, Lieut. Col. Greenberry F. Wiles

THIRD BRIGADE
Col. Adam G. Malloy
17th Wisconsin, Lieut. Col. Thomas McMahon
Worden's Battalion, Maj. Asa Worden

ARTILLERY
    Capt. William S. Williams
    1st Illinois Light Battery D, Capt. Edgar H. Cooper
    1st Michigan Light Battery H, Capt. Marcus D. Elliot
    3rd Ohio Light Battery, Lieut. John Sullivan

FOURTH DIVISION
    Brig. Gen. Walter Q. Gresham

ESCORT
    Company G, 11th Illinois Cavalry, Capt. Stephen S. Tripp

FIRST BRIGADE
    Col. William L. Sanderson
    32nd Illinois, Col. John Logan
    23rd Indiana, Lieut. Col. William P. Davis
    53rd Indiana, Lieut. Col. William Jones
    3rd Iowa (3 companies), Capt. Daniel McLennan
    12th Wisconsin, Col. George E. Bryant

SECOND BRIGADE
    Col. George C. Rodgers
    14th Illinois, Capt. Carlos R. Cox
    15th Illinois, Maj. Rufus C. McEathron
    32nd Illinois, Lieut. Col. George H. English
    41st Illinois, Maj. Robert H. McFadden
    53rd Illinois, Lieut. Col. John W. McClanahan

THIRD BRIGADE
    Col. William Hall
    11th Iowa, Col. John C. Abercrombie
    13th Iowa, Col. John Shane
    15th Iowa, Col. William W. Belknap
    16th Iowa, Lieut. Col. Addison H. Sanders

ARTILLERY
    Capt. Edward Spear
    2nd Illinois Light Battery F, Lieut. Walter H. Powell
    1st Minnesota Battery, Capt. William Z. Clayton
    10th Ohio Light Battery, Capt. Francis Seaman
    15th Ohio Light Battery, Lieut. James Burdick

ARMY OF THE OHIO (TWENTY-THIRD CORPS)
Maj. Gen. John M. Schofield

ESCORT
Company G, 7th Ohio Cavalry, Capt. John A. Asbury

ENGINEER BATTALION
Capt. Oliver S. McClure

FIRST DIVISION
Brig. Gen. Alvin P. Hovey

First Brigade
Col. Richard Barter
120th Indiana, Lieut. Col. Allen W. Prather
124th Indiana, Col. John M. Orr
128th Indiana, Lieut. Col. Jasper Packard

Second Brigade
Col. Peter T. Swaine
123rd Indiana, Lieut. Col. William A. Cullen
129th Indiana, Col. Charles A. Zollinger
130th Indiana, Col. Charles S. Parrish
99th Ohio, Lieut. Col. John E. Cummins

Artillery
23rd Indiana Light Battery, Lieut. Luther S. Houghton
24th Indiana Light Battery, Capt. Alexander Hardy

SECOND DIVISION
Brig. Gen. Milo S. Hascall

First Brigade
Brig. Gen. Joseph A. Cooper
91st Indiana, Col. John Mehringer
25th Michigan, Col. Benjamin F. Orcutt
3rd Tennessee, Col. William Cross
6th Tennessee, Capt. William Ausmus

Second Brigade
Col. William E. Hobson

107th Illinois, Lieut. Col. Uriah M. Laurence
80th Indiana, Lieut. Col. Alfred D. Owen
13th Kentucky, Col. William E. Hobson
23rd Michigan, Lieut. Col. Oliver L. Spaulding
111th Ohio, Col. John R. Bond.
118th Ohio, Capt. Edgar Sowers

THIRD BRIGADE
Col. Silas A. Strickland
14th Kentucky, Col. George W. Gallup
20th Kentucky, Lieut. Col. Thomas B. Waller
27th Kentucky, Lieut. Col. John H. Ward
50th Ohio, Lieut. Col. George R. Elstner

ARTILLERY
Capt. Joseph C. Shields
22nd Indiana Light Battery, Capt. Benjamin F. Denning
1st Michigan Light Battery F, Capt. Byron D. Paddock
19th Ohio Light Battery, Capt. Joseph C. Shields

THIRD DIVISION
Brig. Gen. Jacob D. Cox

FIRST BRIGADE
Col. James W. Reilly
112th Illinois, Lieut. Col. Emery S. Bond
16th Kentucky, Maj. John S. White
100th Ohio, Col. Patrick S. Slevin
104th Ohio, Col. Oscar W. Sterl
8th Tennessee, Col. Felix A. Reeve

SECOND BRIGADE
Col. Daniel Cameron
65th Illinois, Col. William S. Stewart
63rd Indiana, Col. Israel N. Stiles
65th Indiana, Lieut. Col. Thomas Johnson
24th Kentucky, Col. John S. Hurt
103rd Ohio, Col. John S. Casement

THIRD BRIGADE
Col. Robert K. Byrd
11th Kentucky, Col. Palace Love
12th Kentucky, Lieut. Col. Laurence H. Rousseau

1st Tennessee, Col. Robert K. Byrd
5th Tennessee, Col. James T. Shelley

DISMOUNTED CAVALRY BRIGADE
Col. Eugene W. Crittenden
16th Illinois, Capt. Hiram S. Hanchett
12th Kentucky, Lieut. Col. James T. Bramlette

ARTILLERY
Maj. Henry W. Wells
15th Indiana Light Battery, Capt. Alonzo D. Harvey
1st Ohio Light Battery D, Capt. Giles A. Cockerill

CAVALRY CORPS
Brig. Gen. Washington Elliott

ESCORT
Company D, 4th Ohio, Capt. Philip H. Warner

FIRST DIVISION
Brig. Gen. Edward M. McCook

FIRST BRIGADE
Col. Joseph B. Dorr
8th Iowa, Lieut. Col. Horatio G. Barner
4th Kentucky Mounted Infantry, Col. John T. Croxton
2nd Michigan, Lieut. Col. Benjamin Smith
1st Tennessee, Col. James P. Brownlow

SECOND BRIGADE
Lieut. Col. Horace P. Lamson
2nd Indiana, Lieut. Col. David A. Briggs
4th Indiana, Maj. George H. Purdy
1st Wisconsin, Maj. Nathan Paine

THIRD BRIGADE
Stationed at Wauhatchie, Tennessee, and northern Georgia

ARTILLERY
18th Indiana Horse Artillery Battery, Lieut. William B. Rippetoe

SECOND DIVISION
Brig. Gen. Kenner Garrard

First Brigade
- Col. Robert H. G. Minty
- 4th Michigan, Lieut. Col. Josiah B. Park
- 7th Pennsylvania, Col. William B. Sipes
- 4th United States, Capt. James B. McIntyre

Second Brigade
- Col. Eli Long
- 1st Ohio, Col. Beroth B. Eggleston
- 3rd Ohio, Col. Charles B. Seidel
- 4th Ohio, Lieut. Col. Oliver P. Robie

Third Mounted Infantry (Lightning Brigade)
- Col. Abram O. Miller
- 98th Illinois, Lieut. Col. Edward Kitchell
- 123rd Illinois, Lieut. Col. Jonathan Biggs
- 17th Indiana, Lieut. Col. Henry Jordan
- 72nd Indiana, Capt. Adam Pinkerton

CHICAGO BOARD OF TRADE BATTERY
Lieut. George Robinson

THIRD DIVISION
Col. William W. Lowe

First Brigade
- Lieut. Col. Robert Klein
- 3rd Indiana, Maj. Alfred Gaddis
- 5th Iowa, Maj. Harlon Baird

Second Brigade
- Col. Charles C. Smith
- 8th Indiana, Lieut. Col. Fielder A. Jones
- 2nd Kentucky, Lieut. Col. William H. Eifort
- 10th Ohio, Maj. William W. Sanderson

Third Brigade
- Col. Eli H. Murray
- 92nd Illinois Mounted Infantry, Col. Smith D. Adkins
- 3rd Kentucky, Maj. Lewis Wolfley
- 5th Kentucky, Col. Oliver L. Baldwin

Artillery
- 10th Wisconsin Battery, Capt. Yates V. Beebe

CAVALRY DIVISION
Maj. Gen. George Stoneman

ESCORT
Company D, 7th Ohio, Lieut. Samuel Murphy

First Brigade
Col. Israel Garrard
9th Michigan, Col. George S. Acker
7th Ohio, Lieut. Col. George G. Miner

Second Brigade
Col. James Biddle
5th Indiana, Col. Thomas H. Butler
6th Indiana, Lieut. Col. Courtland C. Matson

Third Brigade
Col. Horace Capron
14th Illinois, Lieut. Col. David P. Jenkins
8th Michigan, Lieut. Col. Elisha Mix
McLaughlin's Ohio Squadron, Maj. Richard Rice

Independent Brigade
Col. Alexander W. Holeman
1st Kentucky, Lieut. Col. Silas Adams
11th Kentucky, Lieut. Col. Archibald J. Alexander

Artillery
24th Indiana Battery, Capt. Alexander Hardy

APPENDIX III

CONFEDERATE ORDER OF BATTLE

BATTLE OF KOLB'S FARM
June 22, 1864

ARMY OF TENNESSEE
  Gen. Joseph E. Johnston

HOOD'S ARMY CORPS
  Lieut. Gen. John B. Hood

HINDMAN'S DIVISION
  Maj. Gen. Thomas C. Hindman

Deas's Alabama Brigade
  Brig. Gen. Zachariah C. Deas
  19th Alabama, Col. George R. Kimbrough
  22nd Alabama, Col. Benjamin R. Hart
  25th Alabama, Col. George D. Johnston
  39th Alabama, Col. William C. Clifton
  50th Alabama, Col. John C. Coltart
  17th Alabama Sharpshooters, Capt. James F. Nabers
Manigault's Brigade
  Brig. Gen. Arthur M. Manigault

24th Alabama, Col. Newton N. Davis
28th Alabama, Lieut. Col. William L. Butler
34th Alabama, Col. Julius C. B. Mitchell
10th South Carolina, Col. James Pressley
19th South Carolina, Maj. James L. White

WALTHALL'S MISSISSIPPI BRIGADE
Col. Samuel Benton
24th and 27th Mississippi, Col. Robert P. McKelvaine
29th and 30th Mississippi, Col. William F. Brantley
34th Mississippi, Col. Samuel Benton

TUCKER'S MISSISSIPPI BRIGADE
Col. Jacob H. Sharp
7th Mississippi, Col. William H. Bishop
9th Mississippi, Lieut. Col. Benjamin F. Johns
10th Mississippi, Lieut. Col. George B. Myers
41st Mississippi, Col. J. Byrd Williams
44th Mississippi, Lieut. Col. R. G. Kelsey
9th Mississippi Sharpshooters, Maj. William C. Richards

STEVENSON'S DIVISION
Maj. Gen. Carter L. Stevenson

BROWN'S TENNESSEE BRIGADE
Col. Edwin C. Cook
3rd Tennessee, Lieut. Col. Calvin J. Clack
18th Tennessee, Lieut. Col. William R. Butler
26th Tennessee, Col. Richard M. Saffell
32nd Tennessee, Col. Edwin C. Cook
23rd and 45th Tennessee, Col. Anderson Searcy

CUMMING'S GEORGIA BRIGADE
Col. Elihu P. Watkins (Brig. Gen. Alfred Cumming
    led division's first line)
2nd Georgia State Line, Col. James Wilson
34th Georgia, Maj. John M. Jackson
36th Georgia, Maj. Charles E. Broyles
39th Georgia, Lieut. Col. J. E. B. Jackson
56th Georgia, Col. Elihu P. Watkins

REYNOLD'S BRIGADE
Col. Robert C. Trigg
58th North Carolina, Maj. Thomas J. Dula

60th North Carolina, Col. Washington M. Hardy
54th Virginia, Col. Robert C. Trigg
63rd Virginia, Capt. Connally H. Lynch

PETTUS'S ALABAMA BRIGADE
Col. Charles M. Shelly (Brig. Gen. Edmund W. Pettus led division's second line)
20th Alabama, Col. James M. Dedman
23rd Alabama, Lieut. Col. Joseph B. Bibb
30th Alabama, Col. Charles M. Shelly
31st Alabama, Col. Daniel R. Hundley
46th Alabama, Capt. George E. Brewer

STEWART'S DIVISION
Maj. Gen. Alexander P. Stewart

STOVALL'S GEORGIA BRIGADE
Brig. Gen. Marcellus A. Stovall
1st Georgia State Line, Col. Edward M. Galt
40th Georgia, Col. Abda Johnson
41st Georgia, Maj. Mark S. Nall
42nd Georgia, Col. Robert J. Henderson
43rd Georgia, Lieut. Col. Henry C. Kellogg
52nd Georgia, Capt. John R. Russell

CLAYTON'S ALABAMA BRIGADE
Brig. Gen. Henry D. Clayton
18th Alabama, Col. Peter F. Hunley
32nd and 58th Alabama, Col. Bushrod Jones
36th Alabama, Col. Thomas H. Herndon
38th Alabama, Lieut. Col. W. J. Hearin

GIBSON'S LOUISIANA BRIGADE
Brig. Gen. Randall L. Gibson
1st Louisiana, Maj. S. S. Batchelor
13th Louisiana, Lieut. Col. Francis L. Campbell
16th and 25th Louisiana, Col. Joseph C. Lewis
19th Louisiana, Col. Richard W. Turner
20th Louisiana, Col. Leon von Zinken
14th Battalion Louisiana Sharpshooters, Maj. John E. Austin

BAKER'S ALABAMA BRIGADE
Brig. Gen. Alpheus Baker
37th Alabama, Lieut. Col. Alexander A. Greene

40th Alabama, Col. John H. Higley
42nd Alabama, Lieut. Col. Thomas C. Lanier
54th Alabama, Lieut. Col. John A. Minter

HOOD'S CORPS ARTILLERY
Col. Robert F. Beckham

COURTNEY'S BATTALION
Maj. Alfred R. Courtney
Dent's Alabama Battery, Capt. Staunton H. Dent
Garrity's Alabama Battery, Capt. James Garrity
Douglas's Texas Battery, Capt. James P. Douglas

ELDRIDGE'S BATTALION
Maj. John W. Eldridge
Eufaula Alabama Battery, Capt. McDonald Oliver
Fenner's Louisiana Battery, Capt. Charles E. Fenner
Stanford's Mississippi Battery, Lieut. James S. McCall

JOHNSTON'S BATTALION
Capt. Maximillian van den Corput
Georgia Light Battery, Capt. John B. Rowan
Cherokee Georgia Battery, Capt. Maximillian van den Corput
Marshall's Tennessee Battery, Capt. Lucius G. Marshall

WILLIAMS'S BATTALION
Lieut. Col. Samuel C. Williams
Barbour Alabama Battery, Capt. Reuben F. Kolb
Jefferson Mississippi Battery, Capt. Putnam Darden
Jeffress's Virginia Battery, Capt. William C. Jeffress

BATTLE OF KENNESAW MOUNTAIN
June 27, 1864

ARMY OF TENNESSEE
Gen. Joseph E. Johnston

CHIEF OF STAFF
Brig. Gen. William W. Mackall

CHIEF OF ARTILLERY
Brig. Gen. Francis A. Shoup

CHIEF ENGINEER
Lieut. Col. Stephen W. Presstman

MEDICAL DIRECTOR
Surg. (Maj.) A. J. Foard

CHIEF ORDNANCE OFFICER
Capt. W. D. Humphries

HARDEE'S ARMY CORPS
Lieut. Gen. William J. Hardee

CHEATHAM'S DIVISION
Maj. Gen. Benjamin F. Cheatham

Maney's Tennessee Brigade
Brig. Gen. George E. Maney
1st and 27th Tennessee, Col. Hume R. Feild
4th Confederate, Lieut. Col. Oliver A. Bradshaw
6th and 9th Tennessee, Lieut. Col. John W. Buford
41st Tennessee, Col. James D. Tillman
50th Tennessee, Col. Stephen H. Colms

Strahl's Tennessee Brigade
Brig. Gen. Otho F. Strahl
4th and 5th Tennessee, Col. Jonathan J. Lamb
19th Tennessee, Col. Francis M. Walker
24th Tennessee, Col. John A. Wilson
31st Tennessee, Lieut. Col. Fountain E. P. Stafford
33rd Tennessee, Col. Warner P. Jones

Wright's Tennessee Brigade
Col. John C. Carter
8th Tennessee, Col. John H. Anderson
16th Tennessee, Maj. Benjamin Randals
28th Tennessee, Col. David C. Cook
38th Tennessee, Lieut. Col. Andrew D. Gwynne
51st and 52nd Tennessee, Lieut. Col. John W. Estes

Vaughan's Tennessee Brigade
Brig. Gen. Alfred J. Vaughan Jr.
11th Tennessee, Col. George W. Gordon

12th and 47th Tennessee, Col. William M. Watkins
13th and 154th Tennessee, Col. Michael Magevney Jr.
29th Tennessee, Col. Horace Rice

CLEBURNE'S DIVISION
Maj. Gen. Patrick R. Cleburne

Polk's Brigade
Brig. Gen. Lucius Polk
1st and 15th Arkansas, Lieut. Col. William H. Martin
5th Confederate, Maj. Richard J. Person
2nd Tennessee, Col. William D. Robison
35th and 48th Tennessee, Capt. Henry G. Evans

Govan's Arkansas Brigade
Brig. Gen. Daniel C. Govan
2nd and 24th Arkansas, Col. E. Warfield
5th and 13th Arkansas, Col. John E. Murray
6th and 7th Arkansas, Col. Samuel G. Smith
8th and 19th Arkansas, Col. George F. Baucum
3rd Confederate, Capt. M. H. Dixon

Lowrey's Brigade
Brig. Gen. Mark P. Lowery
16th Alabama, Lieut. Col. Frederick A. Ashford
33rd Alabama, Col. Sam Adams
45th Alabama, Col. Harris D. Lampley
32nd Mississippi, Col. William H. Tison
45th Mississippi, Col. Aaron B. Hardcastle

Granbury's Texas Brigade
Brig. Gen. Hiram M. Granbury
6th and 15th Texas Cavalry, Capt. Rhoads Fisher
7th Texas, Capt. C. E. Talley
10th Texas, Col. Roger Q. Mills
17th and 18th Texas Cavalry, Capt. George D. Manion
24th and 25th Texas Cavalry, Lieut. Col. William M. Neyland

BATE'S DIVISION
Maj. Gen. William B. Bate

Smith's Brigade
Brig. Gen. Thomas B. Smith

37th Georgia, Col. Joseph T. Smith
4th Georgia Sharpshooters, Maj. Theodore D. Caswell
15th and 37th Tennessee, Lieut. Col. Dudley R. Frayser
20th Tennessee, Lieut. Col. William M. Shy
30th Tennessee, Lieut. Col. James J. Turner

Lewis's Kentucky Orphan Brigade
Brig. Gen. Joseph H. Lewis
2nd Kentucky, Col. James W. Moss
4th Kentucky, Lieut. Col. Thomas W. Thompson
5th Kentucky, Lieut. Col. Hiram Hawkins
6th Kentucky, Col. Martin H. Cofer
9th Kentucky, Col. John W. Caldwell

Finley's Florida Brigade
Brig. Gen. Jessie J. Finley
1st and 3rd Florida Cavalry (dismounted), Maj. Glover A. Ball
1st and 4th Florida, Lieut. Col. Edward Badger
6th Florida, Lieut. Col. Daniel L. Kenan
7th Florida, Col. Robert Bullock

WALKER'S DIVISION
Maj. Gen. William H. T. Walker

Mercer's Georgia Brigade
Brig. Gen. Hugh W. Mercer
1st Georgia, Lieut. Col. Charles H. Olmstead
54th Georgia, Lieut. Col. Morgan Rawls
57th Georgia, Lieut. Col. Cininnatus S. Guyton
63rd Georgia, Col. George A. Gordon

Gist's Brigade
Brig. Gen. States R. Gist
8th Georgia Battalion, Lieut. Col. Zachariah L. Watters
46th Georgia, Maj. Samuel J. C. Dunlap
16th South Carolina, Col. James McCullough
24th South Carolina, Col. Ellison Capers

Jackson's Brigade
Brig. Gen. John R. Jackson
47th Georgia, Col. A. C. Edwards
65th Georgia, Capt. William G. Foster
2nd Georgia Sharpshooters, Maj. Richard H. Whiteley

5th Mississippi, Col. John Weir
8th Mississippi, Col. John C. Wilkinson

STEVENS'S GEORGIA BRIGADE
Brig. Gen. Clement H. Stevens
1st Georgia Confederate, Col. George A. Smith
25th Georgia, Col. William J. Winn
29th Georgia, Maj. John J. Owen
30th Georgia, Lieut. Col. James S. Boynton
66th Georgia, Col. James C. Nisbet
1st Georgia Sharpshooters, Maj. Arthur Schaaff

HARDEE'S CORPS ARTILLERY
Col. Melancthon Smith

HOXTON'S BATTALION
Maj. Llewelyn Hoxton
Phelan's Alabama Battery, Capt. John Phelan
Perry's Florida Battery, Capt. Thomas J. Perry
Turner's Mississippi Battery, Capt. William B. Turner

HOTCHKISS'S BATTALION
Maj. Thomas R. Hotchkiss
Goldthwaite's Alabama Battery, Capt. Richard W. Goldthwaite
Key's Arkansas Battery, Capt. Thomas J. Key
Shannon's Mississippi Battery, Lieut. Harvey Shannon

MARTIN'S BATTALION
Maj. Robert Martin
Howell's Georgia Battery, Capt. Evan P. Howell
Bledsoe's Missouri Battery, Capt. Hiram M. Bledsoe
Beauregard's South Carolina Battery, Lieut. Rene Beauregard

COBB'S BATTALION
Maj. Robert Cobb
Gracey's Kentucky Battery, Capt. Frank P. Gracey
Mebane's Tennessee Battery, Capt. J. W. Phillips
Washington Louisiana Battery, Capt. Cuthbert H. Slocomb

PALMER'S BATTALION
Maj. Joseph Palmer
Lumsden's Alabama Battery, Capt. Charles L. Lumsden
Anderson's Georgia Battery, Capt. Ruel W. Anderson
Havis's Georgia Battery, Capt. Minor W. Havis

HOOD'S ARMY CORPS
Lieut. Gen. John B. Hood

HINDMAN'S DIVISION
Maj. Gen. Thomas C. Hindman

Deas's Alabama Brigade
Brig. Gen. Zachariah C. Deas
19th Alabama, Col. George R. Kimbrough
22nd Alabama, Col. Benjamin R. Hart
25th Alabama, Col. George D. Johnston
39th Alabama, Col. William C. Clifton
50th Alabama, Col. John C. Coltart
17th Alabama Sharpshooters, Capt. James F. Nabers

Manigault's Brigade
Brig. Gen. Arthur M. Manigault
24th Alabama, Col. Newton N. Davis
28th Alabama, Lieut. Col. William L. Butler
34th Alabama, Col. Julius C. B. Mitchell
10th South Carolina, Col. James Pressley
19th South Carolina, Maj. James L. White

Walthall's Mississippi Brigade
Col. Samuel Benton
24th and 27th Mississippi, Col. Robert P. McKelvaine
29th and 30th Mississippi, Col. William F. Brantley
34th Mississippi, Col. Samuel Benton

Tucker's Mississippi Brigade
Col. Jacob H. Sharp
7th Mississippi, Col. William H. Bishop
9th Mississippi, Lieut. Col. Benjamin F. Johns
10th Mississippi, Lieut. Col. George B. Myers
41st Mississippi, Col. J. Byrd Williams
44th Mississippi, Lieut. Col. R. G. Kelsey
9th Mississippi Sharpshooters, Maj. William C. Richards

STEVENSON'S DIVISION
Maj. Gen. Carter L. Stevenson

BROWN'S TENNESSEE BRIGADE
    Col. Edwin C. Cook
    3rd Tennessee, Lieut. Col. Calvin J. Clack
    18th Tennessee, Lieut. Col. William R. Butler
    26th Tennessee, Col. Richard M. Saffell
    32nd Tennessee, Col. John P. McGuire
    23rd and 45th Tennessee, Col. Anderson Searcy

CUMMING'S GEORGIA BRIGADE
    Brig. Gen. Alfred Cumming
    2nd Georgia State Line, Col. James Wilson
    34th Georgia, Maj. John M. Jackson
    36th Georgia, Maj. Charles E. Broyles
    39th Georgia, Lieut. Col. J. E. B. Jackson
    56th Georgia, Col. Elihu P. Watkins

REYNOLD'S BRIGADE
    Col. Robert C. Trigg
    58th North Carolina, Maj. Thomas J. Dula
    60th North Carolina, Col. Washington M. Hardy
    54th Virginia, Col. Robert C. Trigg
    63rd Virginia, Capt. Connally H. Lynch

PETTUS'S ALABAMA BRIGADE
    Brig. Gen. Edmund W. Pettus
    20th Alabama, Col. James M. Dedman
    23rd Alabama, Lieut. Col. Joseph B. Bibb
    30th Alabama, Col. Charles M. Shelly
    31st Alabama, Col. Daniel R. Hundley
    46th Alabama, Capt. George E. Brewer

STEWART'S DIVISION
    Maj. Gen. Alexander P. Stewart

STOVALL'S GEORGIA BRIGADE
    Brig. Gen. Marcellus A. Stovall
    1st Georgia State Line, Col. Edward M. Galt
    40th Georgia, Col. Abda Johnson
    41st Georgia, Maj. Mark S. Nall
    42nd Georgia, Col. Robert J. Henderson
    43rd Georgia, Lieut. Col. Henry C. Kellogg
    52nd Georgia, Capt. John R. Russell

CLAYTON'S ALABAMA BRIGADE
   Brig. Gen. Henry D. Clayton
   18th Alabama, Col. Peter F. Hunley
   32nd and 58th Alabama, Col. Bushrod Jones
   36th Alabama, Col. Thomas H. Herndon
   38th Alabama, Lieut. Col. W. J. Hearin

GIBSON'S LOUISIANA BRIGADE
   Brig. Gen. Randall L. Gibson
   1st Louisiana, Maj. S. S. Batchelor
   13th Louisiana, Lieut. Col. Francis L. Campbell
   16th and 25th Louisiana, Col. Joseph C. Lewis
   19th Louisiana, Col. Richard W. Turner
   20th Louisiana, Col. Leon von Zinken
   14th Battalion Louisiana Sharpshooters, Maj. John E. Austin

BAKER'S ALABAMA BRIGADE
   Brig. Gen. Alpheus Baker
   37th Alabama, Lieut. Col. Alexander A. Greene
   40th Alabama, Col. John H. Higley
   42nd Alabama, Lieut. Col. Thomas C. Lanier
   54th Alabama, Lieut. Col. John A. Minter

HOOD'S CORPS ARTILLERY
   Col. Robert F. Beckham

COURTNEY'S BATTALION
   Maj. Alfred R. Courtney
   Dent's Alabama Battery, Capt. Staunton H. Dent
   Garrity's Alabama Battery, Capt. James Garrity
   Douglas's Texas Battery, Capt. James P. Douglas

ELDRIDGE'S BATTALION
   Maj. John W. Eldridge
   Eufaula Alabama Battery, Capt. McDonald Oliver
   Fenner's Louisiana Battery, Capt. Charles E. Fenner
   Stanford's Mississippi Battery, Capt. Thomas J. Stanford

JOHNSTON'S BATTALION
   Capt. Maximillian van den Corput
   Georgia Light Battery, Capt. John B. Rowan
   Cherokee Georgia Battery, Capt. Maximillian van den Corput
   Marshall's Tennessee Battery, Capt. Lucius G. Marshall

Appendix III

WILLIAMS'S BATTALION
   Lieut. Col. Samuel C. Williams
   Barbour Alabama Battery, Capt. Reuben F. Kolb
   Jefferson Mississippi Battery, Capt. Putnam Darden
   Jeffress's Virginia Battery, Capt. William C. Jeffress

POLK'S ARMY CORPS (ARMY OF MISSISSIPPI)
   Maj. Gen. William W. Loring

ESCORT
   Orleans Louisiana Light Horse Cavalry, Capt. Leeds Greenleaf

LORING'S DIVISION
   Brig. Gen. Winfield S. Featherston

FEATHERSTON'S MISSISSIPPI BRIGADE
   Brig. Gen. Winfield S. Featherston
   3rd Mississippi, Col. Thomas A. Mellon
   22nd Mississippi, Maj. Martin A. Oatis
   31st Mississippi, Col. Marcus D. L. Stephens
   33rd Mississippi, Col. Jabez L. Drake
   40th Mississippi, Lieut. Col. George P. Wallace
   1st Mississippi Sharpshooters, Maj. James M. Stigler

ADAM'S MISSISSIPPI BRIGADE
   Brig. Gen. John Adams
   6th Mississippi, Col. Robert Lowry
   14th Mississippi, Lieut. Col. Washington L. Doss
   15th Mississippi, Col. Michael Farrell
   20th Mississippi, Col. William N. Brown
   23rd Mississippi, Col. Joseph M. Wells
   43rd Mississippi, Col. Richard Harrison

SCOTT'S BRIGADE
   Brig. Gen. Thomas M. Scott
   27th Alabama, Col. James Jackson
   35th Alabama, Col. Samuel S. Ives
   49th Alabama, Lieut. Col. John D. Weeden
   55th Alabama, Col. John Snodgrass
   57th Alabama, Col. Charles J. L. Cunningham
   12th Louisiana, Col. Noel L. Nelson

FRENCH'S DIVISION
Maj. Gen. Samuel G. French

Ector's Brigade
Brig. Gen. Matthew D. Ector
29th North Carolina, Col. Bacchus S. Proffit
39th North Carolina, Col. David Coleman
9th Texas, Col. William H. Young
10th Texas Cavalry, Col. C. R. Earp
14th Texas Cavalry, Col. John L. Camp
32nd Texas Cavalry, Col. Julius A. Andrews

Cockrell's Missouri Brigade
Col. Elijah Gates
1st and 4th Missouri, Col. Hugh Garland
2nd and 6th Missouri, Col. Peter C. Fluornoy
3rd and 5th Missouri, Col. James McGowan
1st and 3rd Missouri Calvary (dismounted), Col. Elijah Gates

Sears's Mississippi Brigade
Col. William S. Barry
4th Mississippi, Col. Thomas N. Adaire
35th Mississippi, Col. Reuben H. Shotwell
36th Mississippi, Col. William W. Witherspoon
46th Mississippi, Col. William H. Clark
7th Mississippi Battalion, Capt. W. A. Trotter

WALTHALL'S DIVISION
Maj. Gen. Edward C. Walthall

Reynold's Arkansas Brigade
Brig. Gen. Daniel H. Reynolds
1st Arkansas Mounted Rifles, Col. Lee M. Ramsaur
2nd Arkansas Mounted Rifles, Col. James A. Williamson
4th Arkansas Mounted Rifles, Col. Henry Bunn
9th Arkansas Mounted Rifles, Col. Isaac L. Dunlop
25th Arkansas Mounted Rifles, Col. Charles J. Turnbull

Cantey's Brigade
Col. Edward A. O'Neal
17th Alabama, Col. Virgil S. Murphy
26th Alabama, Maj. David F. Bryan

29th Alabama, Col. John F. Conoley
37th Mississippi, Col. Orlando S. Holland

QUARLES'S BRIGADE
Brig. Gen. William A. Quarles
1st Alabama, Maj. Samuel L. Knox
4th Alabama, Col. Samuel E. Hunter
30th Louisiana, Lieut. Col. Thomas Shields
42nd Tennessee, Col. Isaac N. Hulme
46th and 55th Tennessee, Col. Robert A. Owens
49th Tennessee, Col. William F. Young
53rd Tennessee, Col. John R. White

POLK'S CORPS ARTILLERY
Lieut. Col. Samuel C. Williams

MYRICK'S BATTALION
Maj. John D. Myrick
Pointe Coupee Louisiana Battery, Capt. Alcide Bouanchard
Cowan's Mississippi Battery, Capt. James J. Cowan
Lookout Tennessee Battery, Capt. Robert L. Barry

STORRS'S BATTALION
Maj. George S. Storrs
Ward's Alabama Battery, Capt. John J. Ward
Hoskins's Mississippi Battery, Capt. James A. Hoskins
Guibor's Mississippi Battery, Capt. Henry Guibor

PRESTON'S BATTALION
Maj. William C. Preston
Tarrant's Alabama Battery, Capt. Edward Tarrant
Selden's Alabama Battery, Lieut. Charles W. Lovelace

WADDELL'S BATTALION
Maj. James F. Waddell
Bellamy's Alabama Battery, Capt. Richard H. Bellamy
Emery's Alabama Battery, Capt. Winslow D. Emery
Barrett's Missouri Battery, Capt. Overton W. Barrett

CAVALRY CORPS
Maj. Gen. Joseph Wheeler

MARTIN'S DIVISION
Maj. Gen. William T. Martin

Allen's Alabama Brigade
Brig. Gen. William W. Allen
1st Alabama, Lieut. Col. D. T. Blakey
3rd Alabama, Col. James Hagan
4th Alabama, Col. Alfred A. Russell
7th Alabama, Capt. George Mason
51st Alabama, Col. M. L. Kirkpatrick
12th Alabama Battalion, Capt. Warren S. Reese

Iverson's Brigade
Brig. Gen. Alfred Iverson
1st Georgia, Col. Samuel W. Davitte
2nd Georgia, Col. Charles C. Crews
3rd Georgia, Col. Robert Thompson
4th Georgia, Col. Isaac W. Avery
6th Georgia, Col. John R. Hart

KELLY'S DIVISION
Brig. Gen. John H. Kelly

Anderson's Brigade
Brig. Gen. Robert H. Anderson
3rd Confederate, Lieut. Col. John McCaskill
5th Confederate, Col. Edward Bird
8th Confederate, Lieut. Col. John S. Parker
10th Confederate, Capt. W. J. Vason
12th Confederate, Capt. Charles H. Conner

Dibrell's Tennessee Brigade
Col. George G. Dibrell
4th Tennessee, Col. William S. McLemore
8th Tennessee, Capt. Jefferson Leftwich
9th Tennessee, Col. Jacob B. Biffle
10th Tennessee, Col. William E. De Moss
11th Tennessee, Col. Daniel W. Holman

Williams's Brigade
Brig. Gen. John S. Williams
2nd Kentucky, Maj. Thomas W. Lewis
3rd Kentucky, Col. J. R. Butler
9th Kentucky, Col. William C. P. Breckinridge
2nd Kentucky Battalion, Capt. John B. Dortch

Allison's Tennessee Squadron, Capt. J. S. Rice
Hamilton's Tennessee Battalion, Maj. Joseph Shaw

HANNON'S ALABAMA BRIGADE
Col. Moses W. Hannon
53rd Alabama, Lieut. Col. John F. Gaines
24th Alabama Battalion, Maj. Robert B. Snodgrass

HUMES'S DIVISION
Brig. Gen. William Y. C. Humes

ASHBY'S TENNESSEE BRIGADE
Col. Henry M. Ashby
1st Tennessee, Col. James T. Wheeler
2nd Tennessee, Capt. John H. Kuhn
5th Tennessee, Col. George W. McKenzie
9th Tennessee, Maj. James H. Akin

HARRISON'S BRIGADE
Col. Thomas H. Harrison
3rd Arkansas, Col. Anson W. Hobson
4th Tennessee, Lieut. Col. Paul F. Anderson
8th Texas, Lieut. Col. Gustave Cook
11th Texas, Col. George H. Reeves

JACKSON'S DIVISION
Brig. Gen. William H. Jackson

ARMSTRONG'S MISSISSIPPI BRIGADE
Brig. Gen. Frank C. Armstrong
1st Mississippi, Col. R. A. Pinson
2nd Mississippi, Maj. John J. Perry
28th Mississippi, Col. Peter B. Starke
Ballentine's Mississippi Regiment, Lieut. Col. William L. Maxwell

ROSS'S TEXAS BRIGADE
Brig. Gen. Lawrence S. Ross
1st Texas Legion, Col. Edwin R. Hawkins
3rd Texas Legion, Col. Jiles S. Boggess
6th Texas Legion, Col. Peter F. Ross
9th Texas Legion, Col. Dudley W. Jones

Ferguson's Brigade
    Brig. Gen. Samuel W. Ferguson
    2nd Alabama, Col. John N. Carpenter
    56th Alabama, Col. William Boyles
    9th Mississippi, Col. Horace H. Miller
    11th Mississippi, Col. Robert O. Perrin
    12th Mississippi Battalion, Col. Robert M. Inge
Wheeler's Horse Artillery
    Lieut. Col. Felix H. Robertson
    Georgia Battery, Lieut. Nathan Davis
    Huwald's Tennessee Battery, Lieut. D. Breck Ramsey
    Huggins's Tennessee Battery, Capt. Almaria L. Huggins
    White's Tennessee Battery, Capt. Benjamin F. White
    Wiggins's Arkansas Battery, Lieut. J. Wylie Callaway
Jackson's Division Artillery
    Capt. John Waties
    Columbus Georgia Battery, Capt. Edward Croft
    Missouri Battery, Capt. Houston King
    South Carolina Battery, Lieut. R. B. Waddell

FIRST DIVISION GEORGIA MILITA
Maj. Gen. Gustavus W. Smith

First Brigade
    Brig. Gen. Reuben W. Carswell
    1st Regiment, Col. Edward H. Pottle
    2nd Regiment, Col. James Stapleton
    3rd Regiment, Col. Q. M. Hill
Second Brigade
    Brig. Gen. Pleasant J. Phillips
    4th Regiment, Col. James N. Mann
    5th Regiment, Col. S. S. Stafford
    6th Regiment, Col. J. W. Burney
Third Brigade
    Brig. Gen. Charles D. Anderson
    7th Regiment, Col. Abner Redding
    8th Regiment, Col. William B. Scott
    9th Regiment, Col. J. M. Hill

FOURTH BRIGADE
    Brig. Gen. Henry K. McCay
    10th Regiment, Col. C. M. Davis
    11th Regiment, Col. William T. Toole
    12th Regiment, Col. Richard Sims

NOTES

Preface

1. See Larry Peterson, *Decisions at Perryville: The Twenty-Two Critical Decisions that Defined the Battle* (Knoxville: University of Tennessee Press, 2022) for further discussion.
2. See Larry Peterson, *Decisions of the Atlanta Campaign: The Twenty-One Critical Decisions That Defined the Operation* (Knoxville: University of Tennessee Press, 2019) for a review of the critical decisions of that campaign.

Introduction

1. See Peterson, *Decisions at Perryville*, chapter 1, "The Confederate High Tide" for details concerning the Confederacy's early chance to be victorious.
2. James M. McPherson, *Battle Cry of Freedom: The Civil War Era* (New York: Ballantine Books, 1988), 339–45.
3. McPherson, *Battle Cry of Freedom*, 464–71, 525–35, 538–44, 557–58.
4. McPherson, *Battle Cry of Freedom*, 571–74.
5. McPherson, *Battle Cry of Freedom*, 638–46.

6. McPherson, *Battle Cry of Freedom*, 653–63.
7. Ezra J. Warner, *Generals in Blue: Lives of the Union Commanders* (Baton Rouge: Louisiana State University Press, 1964), 183–86; William S. McFeely, *Grant: A Biography* (New York: W. W. Norton, 1981), 168–69, 171, 173.
8. McFeely, *Grant*, 171, 173.
9. Nathaniel C. Hughes Jr., *The Battle of Belmont: Grant Strikes South* (Chapel Hill: University of North Carolina, 1991), 4–5, 56–57, 82–175.
10. McPherson, *Battle Cry of Freedom*, 396–402.
11. McPherson, *Battle Cry of Freedom*, 406–14.
12. McPherson, *Battle Cry of Freedom*, 416–17.
13. Larry Peterson, *Decisions of the 1862 Kentucky Campaign: The Twenty-Seven Critical Decisions That Defined the Operation* (Knoxville: University of Tennessee Press, 2019), 27–38.
14. Peterson, *Decisions of the 1862 Kentucky Campaign*, 27–62.
15. Peterson, *Decisions of the 1862 Kentucky Campaign*, 75–87.
16. Peterson, *Decisions of the 1862 Kentucky Campaign*, 89–94.
17. McPherson, *Battle Cry of Freedom*, 579–82. Interestingly, Stones has never contained an apostrophe.
18. McPherson, *Battle Cry of Freedom*, 582.
19. McPherson, *Battle Cry of Freedom*, 563, 582.
20. Michael B. Ballard, *Vicksburg: The Campaign That Opened the Mississippi* (Chapel Hill: University of North Carolina Press, 2004), 396–98, 410; *The Collected Works of Abraham Lincoln*, ed. Roy P. Basler (New Brunswick, NJ: Rutgers University Press, 1953), 6:409.
21. Steven E. Woodworth, *Decision in the Heartland: The Civil War in the West* (Westport, CT: Praeger, 2008), 69–70.
22. Woodworth, *Decision in the Heartland*, 73–77.
23. Woodworth, *Decision in the Heartland*, 77–79.
24. Woodworth, *Decision in the Heartland*, 79–80.
25. Woodworth, *Decision in the Heartland*, 80–82.
26. McPherson, *Battle Cry of Freedom*, 675–77; Larry Peterson, *Decisions at Chattanooga: The Nineteen Critical Decisions that Defined the Battle* (Knoxville: University of Tennessee Press, 2018), 22–32.
27. Peterson, *Decisions at Chattanooga*, 38–40.
28. Peterson, *Decisions at Chattanooga*, 69–76.

29. Peterson, *Decisions at Chattanooga*, 83–84; Richard M. McMurry, *Atlanta, 1864: Last Chance for the Confederacy* (Lincoln: University of Nebraska, 2000), 8.
30. US War Department, *The War of the Rebellion: A Compilation of the Official Records of the Union and Confederate Armies* (Washington, DC: United States Government Printing Office, 1880–1901), series 1, vol. 32, pt. 3, p. 13. This source is hereafter cited as *OR*, and all references are to series 1 unless otherwise indicated. Ulysses S. Grant, *Personal Memoirs of U. S. Grant in Two Volumes* (1886; repr., Harrisburg, PA: Archive Society, 1997), 2:114–15; McMurry, *Atlanta, 1864*, 1; Albert Castel, *Decision in the West: The Atlanta Campaign of 1864* (Lawrence: University Press of Kansas, 1992), 62–64. Grant's successful campaigns were the captures of Forts Henry and Donelson, Vicksburg, and Chattanooga.
31. Grant, *Personal Memoirs*, 2:120; William R. Scaife, *The Campaign for Atlanta*, 4th ed. (Cartersville, GA: Civil War Publications, 1993), 4, table of Union command following 15.
32. William T. Sherman, *Memoirs of General William T. Sherman* (1875; repr., Harrisburg, PA: Archive Society, 1997), 2:26; Castel, *Decision in the West*, 91.
33. Sherman, *Memoirs*, 2:31–32; Joseph E. Johnston, *Narrative of Military Operations during the Civil War* (1874; repr., New York: Da Capo, 1959), 298; Scaife, *Campaign for Atlanta*, 18–22, map following 26.
34. Sherman, *Memoirs*, 2:33–34; Castel, *Decision in the West*, 54; Scaife, *Campaign for Atlanta*, 22–24; Peterson, *Decisions of the Atlanta Campaign*, 37–49.
35. McMurry, *Atlanta, 1864*, 70–72.
36. Scaife, *Campaign for Atlanta*, 47; McMurry, *Atlanta, 1864*, 85–86.
37. Scaife, *Campaign for Atlanta*, 47–56, maps following 56; McMurry, *Atlanta, 1864*, 90–92.
38. McMurry, *Atlanta, 1864*, 102–3; Scaife, *Campaign for Atlanta*, 57–58, maps following 66.
39. Scaife, *Campaign for Atlanta*, 59.

Chapter 1

1. Earl J. Hess, *Kennesaw Mountain: Sherman, Johnston, and the Atlanta Campaign* (Chapel Hill: University of North Carolina Press, 2013), 3, 11–12. Hess counts the Kennesaw Mountain Line as the ninth defensive

line established by Johnston. However, Hess on page 3 admits that the Adairsville line was established only for a few hours, so I concur with Stephen Davis, per written communication on August 3, 2021, that Johnston established eight defensive lines from Dalton to Kennesaw Mountain, with Kennesaw Mountain being the eighth one. Scaife, *Campaign for Atlanta*, 57–60, map following 66; Peterson, *Decisions of the Atlanta Campaign*, 75–77; McMurry, *Atlanta, 1864*, 100–103.

2. Ezra J. Warner, *Generals in Gray: Lives of the Confederate Commanders* (Baton Rouge: Louisiana State University Press, 1959), 161–62.

3. Johnston, *Narrative of Military Operations*, 338; Craig L. Symonds, *Joseph E. Johnston: A Civil War Biography* (New York: W. W. Norton, 1992), 307; Hess, *Kennesaw Mountain*, 13–15; Stanley F. Horn, *The Army of Tennessee: A Military History* (New York: Bobbs-Merrill, 1941), 333.

4. Johnston, *Narrative of Military Operations*, 338; Scaife, *Campaign for Atlanta*, 57–60.

5. Johnston, *Narrative of Military Operations*, 338; Scaife, *Campaign for Atlanta*, 57–60.

6. Johnston, *Narrative of Military Operations*, 338; Scaife, *Campaign for Atlanta*, 57–60.

7. Johnston, *Narrative of Military Operations*, 338–39; Symonds, *Joseph E. Johnston*, 308; Hess, *Kennesaw Mountain*, 13; Thomas Lawrence Connelly, *Autumn of Glory: The Army of Tennessee, 1862–1865* (Baton Rouge: Louisiana State University Press, 1971), 358; Scaife, *Campaign for Atlanta*, map following 66; Hess lists the nine defensive lines as (1) Dalton, Rocky Face Ridge (May 8–12); (2) Resaca (May 13–15); (3) Adairsville (May 17); (4) Cassville (May 19); (5) New Hope Church, Pickett's Mill, Dallas (May 25–June 3); (6) Mountain Line (June 5–14); (7) Gilgal Church Line (June 15–16); (8) Mud Creek Line (June 17–18); and (9) Kennesaw Mountain Line (June 19–July 2). See 1 above.

8. Johnston, *Narrative of Military Operations*, 338–39; Maj. George P. Davis, Leslie J. Perry and Joseph W. Kirkley, eds., *The Official Military Atlas of the Civil War* (1891–95; repr., New York: Barnes and Noble, 2003), plates 60-1, 88-2; Scaife, *Campaign for Atlanta*, map following 66; email from Kennesaw Mountain National Battlefield Park (KMNBP) ranger Jay Haney to park volunteer William Gurry, April 4, 2020, describing the history of Kennesaw Spur / Pigeon Hill. Per Christopher Martin and David A. King, authors of *Marcescence: Poems from Gahneesah* (Georgetown, KY: Finishing Line, 2014), "Gahneesah is the Anglicized form of the Cherokee name for Kennesaw Mountain. It means 'burial

ground' or 'place of the dead.'" See "2014 Faculty Bookshelf: *Marcescence: Poems from Gahneesah*," DigitalCommons@Kennesaw State University website, https:/digitalcommons.kennesaw.edu/facbooks2014/24.

9. Hess, *Kennesaw Mountain*, 51; Earl J. Hess, *Fighting for Atlanta: Tactics, Terrain, and Trenches in the Civil War* (Chapel Hill: University of North Carolina Press, 2018), 106, 298. Abatis are cut tree limbs pointed in the direction of the enemy. See Hess, *Kennesaw Mountain*, 27 for comment on rain, and 241, 243–44, 246, 248, 250–51, 254, and 257 for detailed maps of the various trenches.

10. Johnston, *Narrative of Military Operations*, 338–39; Scaife, *Campaign for Atlanta*, 60, map following 66; Sherman, *Memoirs*, 2:56–57.

11. Hess, *Kennesaw Mountain*, 100; Hess, *Fighting for Atlanta*, 101; McMurry, *Atlanta, 1864*, 104; Sherman, *Memoirs*, 2:56.

12. Hess, *Kennesaw Mountain*, 57. Note that Hess labels the hill as Cheatham's Hill (with an apostrophe and *s*), while the National Park Service (NPS) and most other sources name it Cheatham Hill. As a former NPS park ranger myself, I have chosen to use the NPS nomenclature.

13. Hess, *Kennesaw Mountain*, 58.

14. Warner, *Generals in Gray*, 47–48; Christopher Losson, *Tennessee's Forgotten Warriors: Frank Cheatham and His Confederate Division* (Knoxville: University of Tennessee Press, 1989), 9, 20–23.

15. Cheatham recollections, *Supplement to the Official Records of the Union and Confederate Armies* (hereafter referred to as *SOR*), in 2 parts, 68 volumes, (Wilmington, NC; Broadfoot, 1994; pt. 1, vol. 7, p. 143; Hess, *Kennesaw Mountain*, 57–58; Losson, *Tennessee's Forgotten Warriors*, 153; Hess, *Fighting for Atlanta*, 99–100.

16. *SOR*, pt. 1, vol. 7, p. 143; Hess, *Kennesaw Mountain*, 57–58; Hess, *Fighting for Atlanta*, 99–100; Losson, *Tennessee's Forgotten Warriors*, 153.

17. *SOR*, pt. 1, vol. 7, p. 143; Hess, *Kennesaw Mountain*, 57–58; Hess, *Fighting for Atlanta*, 99–100; Losson, *Tennessee's Forgotten Warriors*, 153.

18. *SOR*, pt. 1, vol. 7, p. 143; Hess, *Kennesaw Mountain*, 57–58; Hess, *Fighting for Atlanta*, 99–100; Losson, *Tennessee's Forgotten Warriors*, 153–54.

19. *SOR*, pt. 1, vol. 7, p. 143; Hess, *Kennesaw Mountain*, 57–58; Hess, *Fighting for Atlanta*, 99–100; Losson, *Tennessee's Forgotten Warriors*, 153–54.

20. Hess, *Kennesaw Mountain*, 57–58; Hess, *Fighting for Atlanta*, 99–100; Losson, *Tennessee's Forgotten Warriors*, 153–54.

21. Peterson, *Decisions at Chattanooga*, 51–53.

22. Peterson, *Decisions at Chattanooga*, 51–53.

23. United States Army, *Dictionary of United States Army Terms* (Washington, DC: US Government Printing Office, 1983), 117; Peterson, *Decisions at Chattanooga*, 51–53.

24. *SOR*, pt. 1, vol. 7, p. 143; Hess, *Kennesaw Mountain*, 57–58; Hess, *Fighting for Atlanta*, 99–100; Losson, *Tennessee's Forgotten Warriors*, 153–54.

25. *SOR*, pt. 1, vol. 7, p. 143; Hess, *Kennesaw Mountain*, 57–58; Hess, *Fighting for Atlanta*, 99–100, 123; Losson, *Tennessee's Forgotten Warriors*, 153–54. The history of using the topographical crest is based on a spring 2017 conversation with National Park Service ranger Lee White, a historian at Chickamauga and Chattanooga National Military Park.

26. This will be discussed in regard to critical decision nine, which pertains to some of the Union soldiers establishing a line just below the salient at Cheatham Hill.

27. Hess, *Kennesaw Mountain*, 58; Losson, *Tennessee's Forgotten Warriors*, 154; Hess, *Fighting for Atlanta*, 105.

28. Hess, *Kennesaw Mountain*, 58; Losson, *Tennessee's Forgotten Warriors*, 154; Hess, *Fighting for Atlanta*, 105.

29. Hess, *Kennesaw Mountain*, 58; Losson, *Tennessee's Forgotten Warriors*, 154; Hess, *Fighting for Atlanta*, 105.

30. Hess, *Kennesaw Mountain*, 58; Losson, *Tennessee's Forgotten Warriors*, 154; Hess, *Fighting for Atlanta*, 105.

31. Hess, *Kennesaw Mountain*, 58; Losson, *Tennessee's Forgotten Warriors*, 154; Hess, *Fighting for Atlanta*, 105.

32. Hess, *Kennesaw Mountain*, 61; Losson, *Tennessee's Forgotten Warriors*, 154; Hess, *Fighting for Atlanta*, 105.

33. Lawrence K. Peterson, *Confederate Combat Commander: The Remarkable Life of Brigadier General Alfred Jefferson Vaughan Jr.* (Knoxville: University of Tennessee Press, 2013), 65–66; Jack Coggins, *Arms and Equipment of the Civil War* (1962; repr., Wilmington, NC: Broadfoot, 1990), 67; Christopher Perello, *The Quest for Annihilation: The Role & Mechanics of Battle in the American Civil War* (Bakersfield, CA: Strategy and Tactics, 2009), 123–24.

34. The elevations are taken from the trail map of KMNBP, while the elevation of Marietta is from http//www.Wikipedia, *Marietta, GA*, dated October 19, 2020. See also Richard A. Baumgartner and Larry M.

Strayer, *Kennesaw Mountain, June 1864: Bitter Standoff at the Gibraltar of Georgia* (Huntington, WV: Blue Acorn, 1998), 67.

35. Hess, *Kennesaw Mountain*, 22; Samuel G. French, *Two Wars: The Autobiography & Diary of Gen. Samuel G. French* (1901; repr., Huntington, WV: Blue Acorn, 1999), 203.
36. George S. Storrs, "The Artillery at Kennesaw," *Kennesaw (GA) Gazette*, June 17, 1889, 6–7; Scaife, *Campaign for Atlanta*, 60, 167.
37. Storrs, "Artillery at Kennesaw," 6–7; Scaife, *Campaign for Atlanta*, 60.
38. Storrs, "Artillery at Kennesaw," 6–7; Scaife, *Campaign for Atlanta*, 60.
39. George S. Storrs, "Kennesaw Mountain," *Southern Bivouac* 1, no. 4 (December 1882): 136–37; French, *Two Wars*, 203, 205; Storrs, "Artillery at Kennesaw," 6–7; Hess, *Kennesaw Mountain*, 22; Baumgartner and Strayer, *Kennesaw Mountain, June 1864*, 67.
40. *OR*, vol. 38, pt. 3, pp. 968–69; Storrs, "Artillery at Kennesaw," 6–7; French, *Two Wars*, 203, 205; Hess, *Kennesaw Mountain*, 22; Scaife, *Campaign for Atlanta*, 60; Baumgartner and Strayer, *Kennesaw Mountain, June 1864*, 67.
41. Scaife, *Campaign for Atlanta*, 60; Castel, *Decision in the West*, 287.

Chapter 2

1. Sherman, *Memoirs*, 2:51; Hess, *Kennesaw Mountain*, 13; Horn, *Army of Tennessee*, 334. See chapter 1, note 7 in this work for the nine positions.
2. Sherman, *Memoirs*, 2:56; Horn, *Army of Tennessee*, 334; Hess, *Kennesaw Mountain*, 16. Note that Hess maintains Kennesaw Mountain is 1,808 feet above sea level, a 10-foot difference.
3. Sherman, *Memoirs*, 2:57; Stanley F. Horn, *The Army of Tennessee*, (1941; repr., Norman: University of Oklahoma Press, 1993), 334; Scaife, *Campaign for Atlanta*, 60.
4. Sherman, *Memoirs*, 2:27–28, 57; Horn, *Army of Tennessee*, 334; Scaife, *Campaign for Atlanta*, 60.
5. Sherman, *Memoirs*, 2:27–28, 57; Horn, *Army of Tennessee*, 334; Scaife, *Campaign for Atlanta*, 60.
6. Sherman, *Memoirs*, 2:57; Horn, *Army of Tennessee*, 334; Scaife, *Campaign for Atlanta*, 60; Connelly, *Autumn of Glory*, 338.
7. Sherman, *Memoirs*, 2:57; Scaife, *Campaign for Atlanta*, 60; Hess, *Kennesaw Mountain*, 24–25.

8. Horn, *Army of Tennessee*, 334; Hess, *Kennesaw Mountain*, 16.
9. Johnston, *Narrative of Military Operations*, 338; Connelly, *Autumn of Glory*, 338–59.
10. Johnston, *Narrative of Military Operations*, 338; Connelly, *Autumn of Glory*, 338–59.
11. Johnston, *Narrative of Military Operations*, 338; Connelly, *Autumn of Glory*, 338–59.
12. Johnston, *Narrative of Military Operations*, 338; Connelly, *Autumn of Glory*, 338–59.
13. Johnston, *Narrative of Military Operations*, 338; Connelly, *Autumn of Glory*, 338–59.
14. Johnston, *Narrative of Military Operations*, 338; Connelly, *Autumn of Glory*, 338–59.
15. *OR*, vol. 38, pt. 4, pp. 780–81; Johnston, *Narrative of Military Operations*, 339; Hess, *Kennesaw Mountain*, 25; Stephen Davis, *Texas Brigadier to the Fall of Atlanta: John Bell Hood* (Macon, GA: Mercer University Press, 2019), 209.
16. Hess, *Kennesaw Mountain*, 25.
17. Author's explanation.
18. Nathaniel Cheairs Hughes Jr., *General William J. Hardee: Old Reliable* (Baton Rouge: Louisiana State University Press, 1965), 211; author's conjecture based on interpretation of the situation.
19. *OR*, vol. 38, pt. 4, pp. 780–81; Johnston, *Narrative of Military Operations*, 338; Warner, *Generals in Gray*, 142–43; McMurry, *John Bell Hood and the War for Southern Independence* (Lincoln: University of Nebraska Press, 1992), 10; Stephen M. Hood, *John Bell Hood: The Rise, Fall, and Resurrection of a Confederate General* (El Dorado Hills, CA: Savas Beatie, 2013), 2; Castel, *Decision in the West*, 58–62; Connelly, *Autumn of Glory*, 338–59.
20. *OR*, vol. 38, pt. 4, pp. 780–81; Connelly, *Autumn of Glory*, 339.
21. Scaife, *Campaign for Atlanta*, 60, map following 66; Connelly, *Autumn of Glory*, 339; Hughes, *General William J. Hardee*, 211. Apparently, Johnston favored Hood for important assignments.
22. Scaife, *Campaign for Atlanta*, 60, map following 66; Baumgartner and Strayer, *Kennesaw Mountain, June 1864*, 81 (map); Hess, *Kennesaw Mountain*, 30 (map), 33–35; Hess, *Fighting for Atlanta*, 103; Castel, *Decision in the West*, 293 (map), 294.
23. Scaife, *Campaign for Atlanta*, 67; Hess, *Kennesaw Mountain*, 33–35; Castel, *Decision in the West*, 294.

24. Johnston, *Narrative of Military Operations*, 339; Scaife, *Campaign for Atlanta*, 61.
25. Johnston, *Narrative of Military Operations*, 339; Scaife, *Campaign for Atlanta*, 61.
26. Johnston, *Narrative of Military Operations*, 339; Scaife, *Campaign for Atlanta*, 61.
27. Johnston, *Narrative of Military Operations*, 339–40; McMurry, *Atlanta, 1864*, 105–6; Stephen Davis, *Atlanta Will Fall: Sherman, Joe Johnston, and the Yankee Heavy Battalions* (Wilmington, DE: Scholarly Resources, 2001), 81–82; McMurry, *Atlanta, 1864*, 105–6; Scaife, *Campaign for Atlanta*, 67; Castel, *Decision in the West*, 294.
28. Scaife, *Campaign for Atlanta*, 60–61; Davis, *Atlanta Will Fall*, 82.
29. Scaife, *Campaign for Atlanta*, 60–61; Castel, *Decision in the West*, 292.
30. Scaife, *Campaign for Atlanta*, 60–62, map following 66; Hess, *Kennesaw Mountain*, 28–29; McMurry, *Atlanta, 1864*, 105.
31. *OR*, vol. 38, pt. 3, pp. 814–15; Scaife, *Campaign for Atlanta*, 60–62, map following 66; Hess, *Kennesaw Mountain*, 28–29; McMurry, *Atlanta, 1864*, 105.
32. Castel, *Decision in the West*, 295; Scaife, *Campaign for Atlanta*, 60–62, map following 66; McMurry, *Atlanta, 1864*, 106. McMurry lists the casualties as one thousand in Hood's Corps and three hundred for the Union.
33. Castel, *Decision in the West*, 297; Hess, *Fighting for Atlanta*, 104.
34. Sherman, *Memoirs*, 2:58; McMurry, *Atlanta, 1864*, 106–7.
35. Scaife, *Campaign for Atlanta*, 61–62; Larry J. Daniel, *Conquered: Why the Army of Tennessee Failed* (Chapel Hill: University of North Carolina Press, 2019), 294; Castel, *Decision in the West*, 295; Hess, *Kennesaw Mountain*, 44–45.

Chapter 3

1. McMurry, *Atlanta, 1864*, 107; Peterson, *Decisions of the Atlanta Campaign*, 77–78; Davis, *Texas Brigadier*, 183–84.
2. *OR*, vol. 38, pt. 1, p. 68; Sherman, *Memoirs*, 2:60; Hess, *Kennesaw Mountain*, 62; Baumgartner and Strayer, *Kennesaw Mountain, June 1864*, 96, 98; Castel, *Decision in the West*, 300–302.
3. *OR*, vol. 38, pt. 3, p. 552; Castel, *Decision in the West*, 300–301.
4. *OR*, vol. 38, pt. 3, p. 552; Castel, *Decision in the West*, 301.

5. Sherman, *Memoirs*, 2:60; Hess, *Kennesaw Mountain*, 62.
6. *OR*, vol. 38, pt. 1, p. 68; Sherman, *Memoirs*, 2:60.
7. Castel, *Decision in the West*, 301.
8. Castel, *Decision in the West*, 301; Scaife, *Campaign for Atlanta*, 62.
9. *OR*, vol. 38, pt. 4, p. 492; Baumgartner and Strayer, *Kennesaw Mountain, June 1864*, 98.
10. Hess, *Fighting for Atlanta*, 2–3, 111–12; Steven E. Woodworth, *Sherman* (New York: Palgrave McMillian, 2009), 117–18; Lloyd Lewis, *Sherman: Fighting Prophet* (New York: Konecky and Konecky, 1932), 175, 198, 376.
11. Lewis, *Sherman: Fighting Prophet*, 376 comments that it was the first time Sherman had ordered an attack, but it appears that Resaca was first.
12. *OR*, vol. 38, pt. 1, p. 68; *OR*, vol. 38, pt. 4, pp. 582, 588; Sherman, *Memoirs*, 2:60; Scaife, *Campaign for Atlanta*, 63; Castel, *Decision in the West*, 301; McMurry, *Atlanta, 1864*, 107–8; Peterson, *Decisions of the Atlanta Campaign*, 79.
13. *OR*, vol. 38, pt. 4, p. 588; Sherman, *Memoirs*, 2:60; Baumgartner and Strayer, *Kennesaw Mountain, June 1864*, 98; Woodworth, *Sherman*, 118; Lewis, *Sherman: Fighting Prophet*, 376.
14. Baumgartner and Strayer, *Kennesaw Mountain, June 1864*, 98; Scaife, *Campaign for Atlanta*, 64; Hess, *Fighting for Atlanta*, 112.
15. Scaife, *Campaign for Atlanta*, 64, map following 66; Baumgartner and Strayer, *Kennesaw Mountain, June 1864*, 142 (map); Hess, *Fighting for Atlanta*, 115 (map), 120–21.
16. Scaife, *Campaign for Atlanta*, 64, map following 66; Baumgartner and Strayer, *Kennesaw Mountain, June 1864*, 142 (map); Hess, *Fighting for Atlanta*, 115 (map), 117–19.
17. Baumgartner and Strayer, *Kennesaw Mountain, June 1864*, 114 (map); Scaife, *Campaign for Atlanta*, 63, map following 66; Hess, *Fighting for Atlanta*, 115 (map), 113; McMurry, *Atlanta, 1864*, 86; Kennesaw Spur information from email from William Gurry forwarded to me from KMNBP ranger Jay Haney on April 4, 2020. Kennesaw was originally spelled with one *n*, but I have chosen, for consistency, to use the modern spelling throughout.
18. *OR*, vol. 38, pt. 4, p. 589; John M. Schofield, *Forty-Six Years in the Army* (1897; repr., Harrisburg, PA: Archive Society, 1997), 144; Castel, *Decision in the West*, 304; McMurry, *Atlanta, 1864*, 86; Hess, *Fighting for Atlanta*, 112; Hess, *Kennesaw Mountain*, 63–64.

19. *OR*, vol. 38, pt. 3, pp. 98–99; Hess, *Fighting for Atlanta*, 117; Castel, *Decision in the West*, 307; Hess, *Kennesaw Mountain*, 66.
20. Perello, *Quest for Annihilation*, 72–73; Coggins, *Arms and Equipment of the Civil War*, 23–24; Castel, *Decision in the West*, 307; Hess, *Kennesaw Mountain*, 96, 111–14; Hess, *Fighting for Atlanta*, 117–18, 120.
21. Perello, *Quest for Annihilation*, 72–73; Coggins, *Arms and Equipment of the Civil War*, 23–24; Castel, *Decision in the West*, 307; Hess, *Kennesaw Mountain*, 96, 111–14; Hess, *Fighting for Atlanta*, 117–18, 120.
22. Perello, *Quest for Annihilation*, 72–73; Coggins, *Arms and Equipment of the Civil War*, 23–24; Castel, *Decision in the West*, 307; Hess, *Kennesaw Mountain*, 96, 111–14; Hess, *Fighting for Atlanta*, 117–18, 120.
23. Perello, *Quest for Annihilation*, 72–73; Coggins, *Arms and Equipment of the Civil War*, 23–24; Castel, *Decision in the West*, 307; Hess, *Kennesaw Mountain*, 96, 111–14; Hess, *Fighting for Atlanta*, 117–18, 120.
24. Perello, *Quest for Annihilation*, 72–73; Coggins, *Arms and Equipment of the Civil War*, 23–24; Castel, *Decision in the West*, 307; Hess, *Kennesaw Mountain*, 96, 111–13; Hess, *Fighting for Atlanta*, 117–18, 120.
25. Perello, *Quest for Annihilation*, 72–73; Coggins, *Arms and Equipment of the Civil War*, 23–24; Castel, *Decision in the West*, 307; Hess, *Kennesaw Mountain*, 96, 111–14; Hess, *Fighting for Atlanta*, 117–18, 120.
26. Hess, *Kennesaw Mountain*, 96, 100; Scaife, *Campaign for Atlanta*, 64, map following 66.
27. Hess, *Kennesaw Mountain*, 77; Castel, *Decision in the West*, 311; Scaife, *Campaign for Atlanta*, map following 66.
28. Hess, *Kennesaw Mountain*, 79–90; Scaife, *Campaign for Atlanta*, map following 66.
29. Hess, *Kennesaw Mountain*, 88–95; Scaife, *Campaign for Atlanta*, map following 66.
30. Scaife, *Campaign for Atlanta*, map following 66; Baumgartner and Strayer, *Kennesaw Mountain, June 1864*, 142 (map); Hess, *Kennesaw Mountain*, 99 (map), 117 (map); J. B. Work, Map of the Dead Angle, Cheatham's Hill, Kennesaw Mountain, GA., June 27 to July 2–3, 1864, measured September 21, 1902, compiled November 28, 1902, *Confederate Veteran Papers*, Box 1, David M. Rubenstein Rare Book and Manuscript Library, Duke University, Durham, NC.
31. Scaife, *Campaign for Atlanta*, map following 66; Baumgartner and Strayer, *Kennesaw Mountain, June 1864*, 142 (map); Hess, *Kennesaw*

Mountain, 99, (map), 116–17, 117 (map); Work, Map of the Dead Angle. Also see appendix I, Stop 5B in this work for McCook's possible oration prior to his assault.

32. Hess, *Kennesaw Mountain*, 96–112, 279n4; Scaife, *Campaign for Atlanta*, 62–65, map following 66; Hess, *Fighting for Atlanta*, 118.

33. French, *Two Wars*, 211; Peterson, *Confederate Combat Commander*, 178; Baumgartner and Strayer, *Kennesaw Mountain, June 1864*, 129–30; Scaife, *Campaign for Atlanta*, 63; Hess, *Kennesaw Mountain*, 110.

34. Work, Map of the "Dead Angle; Scaife, *Campaign for Atlanta*, map following 66; Baumgartner and Strayer, *Kennesaw Mountain, June 1864*, 142 (map); Hess, *Kennesaw Mountain*, 114–27. See appendix I, Stop 5B in this work for the verse from Horatius.

35. Work, Map of the Dead Angle; Scaife, *Campaign for Atlanta*, map following 66; Baumgartner and Strayer, *Kennesaw Mountain, June 1864*, 142 (map); Hess, *Kennesaw Mountain*, 127–31.

36. Alfred J. Vaughan Jr., *Personal Record of the Thirteenth Regiment, Tennessee Infantry, C.S.A.* (Memphis: S. C. Toof, 1897), 33; Peterson, *Confederate Combat Commander*, 179.

37. Sam Watkins, *Company Aytch, or A Side Show of the Big Show*, ed. M. Thomas Inge (1882; repr., New York: Penguin Putnam, 1999), 133.

38. *OR*, vol. 38, pt. 3, pp. 113–15; Castel, *Decision in the West*, 320; Hess, *Kennesaw Mountain*, 154; McMurry, *Atlanta, 1864*, 109; Peterson, *Decisions of the Atlanta Campaign*, 81; Peterson, *Confederate Combat Commander*, 179–80.

39. *OR*, vol. 38, pt. 4, p. 610; Hess, *Kennesaw Mountain*, 124; Baumgartner and Strayer, *Kennesaw Mountain, June 1864*, 165.

40. *OR*, vol. 38, pt. 1, pp. 692–93, 711, 724; James T. Holmes, *Battle of Kennesaw Mountain: The Memoir of Colonel James T. Holmes, 52nd Ohio Volunteer Infantry*, ed. Garth D. Bishop (Jefferson, NC: McFarland, 2018), 183; Hess, *Fighting for Atlanta*, 121–24; Hess, *Kennesaw Mountain*, 126–27; Peterson, *Confederate Combat Commander*, 180.

41. Hess, *Kennesaw Mountain*, 165; Baumgartner and Strayer, *Kennesaw Mountain, June 1864*, 172.

42. Hess, *Kennesaw Mountain*, 165; Baumgartner and Strayer, *Kennesaw Mountain, June 1864*, 172.

43. Hess, *Kennesaw Mountain*, 165; Baumgartner and Strayer, *Kennesaw Mountain, June 1864*, 172.

44. Losson, *Tennessee's Forgotten Warriors*, 161.

45. Losson, *Tennessee's Forgotten Warriors*, 161; Hess, *Kennesaw Mountain*, 181.
46. Watkins, *Company Aytch*, 136; Hess, *Kennesaw Mountain*, 182–83; Losson, *Tennessee's Forgotten Warriors*, 161. The entrance to this tunnel can be seen today below the Illinois Monument at Cheatham Hill in KMNBP.
47. Watkins, *Company Aytch*, 136; Losson, *Tennessee's Forgotten Warriors*, 161; Hess, *Kennesaw Mountain*, 178–79; Baumgartner and Strayer, *Kennesaw Mountain, June 1864*, 172–73.
48. Sherman, *Memoirs*, 2:61.
49. William T. Sherman, *Home Letters of General Sherman*, ed. M. A. De Wolfe Howe, (New York: Charles Scribner's Sons, 1909), 299–301; Baumgartner and Strayer, *Kennesaw Mountain, June 1864*, 165–66; Castel, *Decision in the West*, 321; Hess, *Kennesaw Mountain*, 162.

Chapter 4

1. Sherman, *Memoirs*, 2:61–62; Castel, *Decision in the West*, 322; McMurry, *Atlanta, 1864*, 110.
2. *OR*, vol. 38, pt. 4, p. 629; Castel, *Decision in the West*, 322–23.
3. Hess, *Kennesaw Mountain*, 188.
4. Hess, *Kennesaw Mountain*, 188.
5. Sherman, *Memoirs*, 2:61–62; Hess, *Kennesaw Mountain*, 188.
6. *OR*, vol. 38, pt. 4, p. 635; Sherman, *Memoirs*, 2:61–62; Hess, *Kennesaw Mountain*, 188–91.
7. Hess, *Kennesaw Mountain*, 191, 197; Baumgartner and Strayer, *Kennesaw Mountain, June 1864*, 177.
8. *OR*, vol. 38, pt. 4, pp. 643–46, 805; *OR*, vol. 39, pt. 2, p. 655; Castel, *Decision in the West*, 379.
9. Johnston, *Narrative of Military Operations*, 344; Losson, *Tennessee's Forgotten Warriors*, 162–63; Baumgartner and Strayer, *Kennesaw Mountain, June 1864*, 173–76; Castel, *Decision in the West*, 323–24.
10. *OR*, vol. 52, pt. 2, pp. 704–7; *OR*, vol. 38, pt. 5, p. 860; Davis, *Texas Brigadier*, 199–200; Peterson, *Decisions of the Atlanta Campaign*, 83.
11. Sherman, *Memoirs*, 2:62; Lewis, *Sherman: Fighting Prophet*, 379; Woodworth, *Sherman*, 119; Robert D. Jenkins Sr., *To the Gates of Atlanta: From Kennesaw Mountain to Peach Tree Creek, 1–19 July 1964* (Macon, GA: Mercer University Press, 2015), 20–21; McMurry, *Atlanta, 1864*, 114.

Chapter 5

1. See Peterson, *Decisions of the Atlanta Campaign* for discussion of critical decisions affecting the initiation of that campaign. Hess, *Kennesaw Mountain*, 13.
2. William T. Sherman to Ellen Sherman, June 29, 1864, in *Home Letters of General Sherman*, ed. Howe; Davis, *Texas Brigadier*, 196; Scaife, *Campaign for Atlanta*, 15, and tables following 15; McPherson, *Battle Cry of Freedom*, 733.
3. *OR*, vol. 38, pt. 5, p. 946; McPherson, *Battle Cry of Freedom*, 733; written correspondence with Stephen Davis, August 3, 2021. Casualty numbers can vary significantly depending on the source.
4. Peterson, *Decisions of the Atlanta Campaign*, 107–11; McMurry, *Atlanta, 1864*, 175–76.
5. Sherman, *Memoirs*, 2:65–66; Johnston, *Narrative of Military Operations*, 345; Scaife, *Campaign for Atlanta*, 67–68, map following 74; Connelly, *Autumn of Glory*, 362; Castel, *Decision in the West*, 330–32; Jenkins, *To the Gates of Atlanta*, 22–29; McMurry, *Atlanta, 1864*, 114.
6. Johnston, *Narrative of Military Operations*, 345; Sherman, *Memoirs*, 2:66; Scaife, *Campaign for Atlanta*, 69–70, map following 74; William R. Scaife, *The Chattahoochee River Line: An American Maginot* (Cartersville, GA: Civil War Publications, 2004), 1–26 and maps following 26; Castel, *Decision in the West*, 332, 334; Jenkins, *To the Gates of Atlanta*, 93–94.
7. Sherman, *Memoirs*, 2:68–69; Johnston, *Narrative of Military Operations*, 346–47; McMurry, *Atlanta, 1864*, 115–17; Scaife, *Campaign for Atlanta*, 72–74, map following 74; Jenkins, *To the Gates of Atlanta*, 1106–19.
8. *OR*, vol. 38, pt. 5, p. 885; Johnston, *Narrative of Military Operations*, 348–49; Castel, *Decision in the West*, 360–62; Connelly, *Autumn of Glory*, 398–402.
9. McMurry, *Atlanta, 1864*, 146–47; Daniel, *Conquered*, 298–99; Steven E. Woodworth, *Nothing but Victory: The Army of the Tennessee, 1861–1865* (New York: Alfred A. Knopf, 2005), 530.
10. Sherman, *Memoirs*, 2:72–74; Scaife, *Campaign for Atlanta*, 78–83, map following 83; Lewis, *Sherman: Fighting Prophet*, 383–84. For a very detailed description of the battle, see Robert D. Jenkins Sr., *The Battle of Peach Tree Creek: Hood's First Sortie, 20 July 1864* (Macon, GA: Mercer University Press, 2013).
11. Scaife, *Campaign for Atlanta*, 85–92 and map following 92; McMurry,

Atlanta, 1864, 152–55; Davis, *Texas Brigadier*, 305; Woodworth, *Nothing but Victory*, 540–68.

12. Scaife, *Campaign for Atlanta*, 85–92 and map following 92; McMurry, *Atlanta, 1864*, 152–55; Woodworth, *Nothing but Victory*, 540–568.

13. *OR*, vol. 38, pt. 5, p. 919; Scaife, *Campaign for Atlanta*, 93–98 and map following 98; Woodworth, *Nothing but Victory*, 572–76; Castel, *Decision in the West*, 425–34.

14. Scaife, *Campaign for Atlanta*, 93–98, and map following 98; Castel, *Decision in the West*, 170–73.

15. Scaife, *Campaign for Atlanta*, 93–98 and map following 98; Castel, *Decision in the West*, 170–73.

16. Sherman, *Memoirs*, 2:171–72; Castel, *Decision in the West*, 553–55; Lewis, *Sherman: Fighting Prophet*, 430–31.

17. Daniel, *Conquered*, 315–22; Connelly, *Autumn of Glory*, 480–506.

18. Daniel, *Conquered*, 322–24; Connelly, *Autumn of Glory*, 506–12.

19. *OR*, vol. 44, p. 783; Sherman, *Memoirs*, 2:171–220; Woodworth, *Sherman*, 152–59.

20. Sherman, *Memoirs*, 2:224; Woodworth, *Sherman*, 160–63; Woodworth, *Nothing but Victory*, 607–36.

21. McPherson, *Battle Cry of Freedom*, 844–50; Chris Calkins, *Lee's Retreat: A History and Field Guide* (Richmond, VA: Page One, 2000), 7–83.

22. Woodworth, *Nothing but Victory*, 634–37; Woodworth, *Sherman*, 162–63; Connelly, *Autumn of Glory*, 534.

23. Charles Higham, *Murdering Mr. Lincoln: A New Detection of the 19th Century's Most Famous Crime* (Beverly Hills, CA: New Millennium, 2004), 215; McPherson, *Battle Cry of Freedom*, 853.

Appendix I

1. Johnston, *Narrative of Military Operations*, 338–39.
2. http//www.campmcdonaldpark.org., established 2010.
3. Sherman, *Memoirs*, 2:10–11, 54.
4. Scaife, *Campaign for Atlanta*, 57–60.
5. McMurry, *Atlanta, 1864*, 102–3.
6. John B. Hood, *Advance and Retreat: Personal Experiences in the United States and Confederate States Armies* (1880; repr., New York: Da Capo, 1993), 125; Hess, *Kennesaw Mountain*, 40–44.

7. Scaife, *Campaign for Atlanta*, 61–62.
8. *OR*, vol. 38, pt. 3, pp. 814–15.
9. Johnston, *Narrative of Military Operations*, 339–40.
10. Sherman, *Memoirs*, 2:60–61.
11. Johnston, *Narrative of Military Operations*, 344.
12. Johnston, *Narrative of Military Operations*, 344.
13. Hess, *Kennesaw Mountain*, 116.
14. Hess, *Kennesaw Mountain*, 116; Thomas B. Macaulay, *Critical, Historical and miscellaneous Essays and Poems,* 3 vol.s (New York: A. L. Burt, n.d.), 765–71.
15. Hess, *Kennesaw Mountain*, 135–36.
16. Hess, *Fighting for Atlanta*, 99–100.
17. Hess, *Kennesaw Mountain*, 97, 111-12.
18. Losson, *Tennessee's Forgotten Warriors*, 155–57.
19. Vaughan, *Personal Record*, 33.
20. Watkins, *Company Aytch*, 132–33.
21. *OR*, vol. 38, pt. 1, p. 721.
22. Hess, *Kennesaw Mountain*, 182–83.
23. Johnston, *Narrative of Military Operations*, 341–42.
24. French, *Two Wars*, 206, 208 (picture on 207).
25. *OR*, vol. 38, pt. 3, pp. 178–79.
26. Johnston, *Narrative of Military Operations*, 344–45.
27. Sherman, *Memoirs*, 2:61–62.

BIBLIOGRAPHY

Primary Sources

Connally, Major James A. *Three Years in the Army of the Cumberland: The Letters and Diary of Major James A. Connally.* Edited by Paul M. Angle. Indianapolis: University of Indiana Press, 1996.

Davis, George P., Leslie J. Perry, and Joseph W. Kirkley, eds. *The Official Military Atlas of the Civil War.* 1891–95. Reprint. New York: Barnes and Noble, 2003.

French, Samuel G. *Two Wars: The Autobiography & Diary of Gen. Samuel G. French.* 1901. Reprint. Huntington, WV: Blue Acorn, 1999.

Grant, Ulysses S. *Personal Memoirs of U. S. Grant in Two Volumes.* 2 vols. 1886. Reprint. Harrisburg, PA: Archive Society, 1997.

Harley, Stanard C. "A Johnny Reb Writes." Washington, DC: *National Tribune*, June 11, 1914.

Holmes, James T. *Movements and Positions in the Battle of Kennesaw Mountain: The Memoir of Colonel James T. Holmes, 52d Ohio Volunteer Infantry.* Edited by Garth D. Bishop. Jefferson, NC: McFarland, 2018.

Hood, John B. *Advance and Retreat: Personal Experiences in the United States and Confederates States Armies.* 1880. Reprint. New York: Da Capo, 1993.

Hood, Stephen M., ed. *The Lost Papers of Confederate General John Bell Hood.* El Dorado Hills, CA: Savas Beatie, 2015.

Jackman, John S. *Diary of a Confederate Soldier: John S. Jackman of the Orphan Brigade.* Edited by William C. Davis. Columbia: University of South Carolina Press, 1990.

Johnston, Joseph E. *Narrative of Military Operations during the Civil War.* 1874. Reprint. New York: Da Capo, 1959.

Macaulay, Thomas B. *Critical, Historical, and Miscellaneous Essays and Poems.* 3 vols. New York: A. L. Burt, n.d.

Manigault, Arthur. *A Carolinian Goes to War.* Edited by R. Lockwood Tower. 1983. Reprint. Columbia: University of South Carolina Press, 1992.

Nisbet, James Cooper. *Four Years on the Firing Line.* Edited by Bell I. Wiley. Wilmington, NC: Broadfoot, 1987.

Schofield, John M. *Forty-Six Years in the Army.* 1897. Reprint. Harrisburg, PA: Archive Society, 1997.

Sherman, William T. "The Grand Strategy of the War of the Rebellion." *Century Magazine,* February 1888. 253.

———. *Home Letters of General Sherman.* Edited by M. A. De Wolfe Howe. New York: Charles Scribner's Sons, 1909.

———. *Memoirs of General William T. Sherman.* 2 vols. 1875. Reprint. New York: D. Appleton, 1997.

Stephenson, Philip Daingerfield. *The Civil War Memoir of Philip Daingerfield Stephenson, D.D.* Edited by Nathaniel Cheairs Hughes Jr. Conway, AR: University of Central Arkansas Press, 1995.

Stone, Henry. "Opening the Campaign." *Papers of the Military Historical Society of Massachusetts,* 3:399.

Storrs, George S. "The Artillery at Kennesaw." *Kennesaw (GA) Gazette,* June 17, 1889, 6–7.

———. "Kennesaw Mountain." *Southern Bivouac* 1, no. 4 (December 1882), 136–37.

Sykes, Columbus. *Letter of May 29, 1864.* Library, Kennesaw Mountain National Battlefield Park, Kennesaw, GA.

United States Marine Corps. *Operations Manuel, 7-21.* Washington, D.C: United States Government Printing Office, 2011.

US Department of the Army. *Field Manual 3-0.* Washington, DC: United States Government Printing Office, 2011.

US Department of the Army. *Field Manual 3-90-1*. Washington, DC: United States Government Printing Office, 2013.

US War Department. *The War of the Rebellion: A Compilation of the Official Records of the Union and Confederate Armies*. 128 vols. Series 1. Washington, DC: United States Government Printing Office, 1880–1901.

Vaughan, Alfred J., Jr. *Personal Record of the Thirteenth Regiment, Tennessee Infantry, C.S.A.* Memphis: S. C. Toof, 1897.

Watkins, Sam. *Company Aytch, or A Side Show of the Big Show*. Edited by M. Thomas Inge. 1882. Reprint. New York: Penguin Putnam, 1999.

Secondary Sources

Ballard, Michael B. *Vicksburg: The Campaign That Opened the Mississippi*. Chapel Hill: University of North Carolina Press, 2004.

Baumgartner, Richard A., and Larry M. Strayer. *Kennesaw Mountain, June 1864: Bitter Standoff at the Gibraltar of Georgia*. Huntington, WV: Blue Acorn, 1998.

Black, Robert C. *The Railroads of the Confederacy*. Chapel Hill: University of North Carolina Press, 1998.

Calkins, Chris. *Lee's Retreat: A History and Field Guide*. Richmond, VA: Page One, 2000.

Castel, Albert. *Decision in the West: The Atlanta Campaign of 1864*. Lawrence: University Press of Kansas, 1992.

Clark, John E. *Railroads in the Civil War: The Impact of Management on Victory and Defeat*. Baton Rouge: Louisiana State University Press, 2001.

Coggins, Jack. *Arms and Equipment of the Civil War*. 1962. Reprint. Wilmington, NC: Broadfoot, 1990.

Connelly, Thomas Lawrence. *Autumn of Glory: The Army of Tennessee, 1862–1865*. Baton Rouge: Louisiana State University Press, 1971.

Daniel, Larry J. *Conquered: Why the Army of Tennessee Failed*. Chapel Hill: University of North Carolina Press, 2019.

———. *Days of Glory: The Army of the Cumberland, 1861–1865*. Baton Rouge: Louisiana State University Press, 2004.

———. *Soldiering in the Army of Tennessee: A Portrait of Life in a Confederate Army*. Chapel Hill: University of North Carolina Press, 1991.

Davis, Stephen. *Atlanta Will Fall: Sherman, Joe Johnston, and the Yankee Heavy Battalions*. Wilmington, DE: Scholarly Resources, 2001.

---. *A Long and Bloody Task: The Atlanta Campaign from Dalton through Kennesaw Mountain to the Chattahoochee River, May 5–July 18, 1864.* El Dorado Hills, CA: Savas Beatie, 2016.

---. *Texas Brigadier to the Fall of Atlanta: John Bell Hood.* Macon, GA: Mercer University Press, 2019.

Davis, William C., ed. *The Civil War.* 27 vols. Alexandria, VA: Time Life Books, 1983–87.

---. *Jefferson Davis: The Man and His Hour.* Baton Rouge: Louisiana State University Press, 1991.

Elliott, Sam Davis. *Soldier of Tennessee: General Alexander P. Stewart and the Civil War in the West.* Baton Rouge: Louisiana State University Press, 1999.

Hallock, Judith Lee. *Braxton Bragg and Confederate Defeat.* Vol. 2. Tuscaloosa: University of Alabama Press, 1991.

Hess, Earl J. *Civil War Infantry Tactics: Training, Combat, and Small-Unit Effectiveness.* Baton Rouge: Louisiana State University Press, 2015.

---. *Fighting for Atlanta: Tactics, Terrain, and Trenches in the Civil War.* Chapel Hill: University of North Carolina Press, 2018.

---. *Kennesaw Mountain: Sherman, Johnston, and the Atlanta Campaign.* Chapel Hill: University of North Carolina Press, 2013.

Hewitt, Lawrence Lee, and Arthur W. Bergeron Jr., eds. *Confederate Generals in the Western Theater.* Vols. 1 and 2. Knoxville: University of Tennessee Press, 2010.

Higham, Charles. *Murdering Mr. Lincoln: A New Detection of the 19th Century's Most Famous Crime.* Beverly Hills, CA: New Millennium, 2004.

Hood, Stephen M. *John Bell Hood: The Rise, Fall, and Resurrection of a Confederate General.* El Dorado Hills, CA: Savas Beatie, 2013.

Horn, Stanley F. *The Army of Tennessee: A Military History.* New York: Bobbs-Merrill, 1941.

Hughes, Nathaniel Cheairs, Jr. *The Battle of Belmont: Grant Strikes South.* Chapel Hill: University of North Carolina, 1991.

---. *General William J. Hardee: Old Reliable.* Baton Rouge: Louisiana State University Press, 1965.

Jenkins, Robert D., Sr. *The Battle of Peach Tree Creek: Hood's First Sortie, 20 July 1864.* Macon, GA: Mercer University Press, 2013.

---. *To the Gates of Atlanta: From Kennesaw Mountain to Peach Tree Creek, 1–19 July 1864.* Macon, GA: Mercer University Press, 2015.

Jones, Archer. *Civil War Command & Strategy: The Process of Victory and Defeat.* New York: Free Press, 1992.

Lewis, Lloyd. *Sherman: Fighting Prophet.* New York: Konecky and Konecky, 1932.

Lincoln, Abraham. *The Collected Works of Abraham Lincoln.* 9 vols. Edited by Roy P. Basler. New Brunswick, NJ: Rutgers University Press, 1953.

Lindsley, John B., ed. *The Military Annals of Tennessee: Confederate.* Nashville: J. M. Lindsley, 1886.

Losson, Christopher. *Tennessee's Forgotten Warriors: Frank Cheatham and His Confederate Division.* Knoxville: University of Tennessee Press, 1989.

McFeely, William S. *Grant: A biography.* New York: W. W. Norton, 1981.

McMurry, Richard M. *Atlanta, 1864: Last Chance for the Confederacy.* Lincoln: University of Nebraska Press, 2001.

———. *John Bell Hood and the War for Southern Independence.*, Lincoln: University of Nebraska Press, 1992.

———. *Two Great Rebel Armies, An Essay in Confederate Military History.* Chapel Hill: The University of North Carolina Press, 1989.

McPherson, James M. *Battle Cry of Freedom: The Civil War Era.* New York: Ballantine Books, 1988.

Parks, Joseph H. *General Leonidas Polk, C.S.A.: The Fighting Bishop.* Baton Rouge: Louisiana State University Press, 1962.

Perello, Christopher. *The Quest for Annihilation: The Role & Mechanics of Battle in the American Civil War.* Bakersfield, CA: Strategy and Tactics, 2009.

Peterson, Larry. *Decisions at Chattanooga: The Nineteen Critical Decisions That Defined the Battle.* Knoxville: University of Tennessee Press, 2018.

———. *Decisions at Perryville: The Twenty-Two Critical Decisions That Defined the Battle.* Knoxville: University of Tennessee Press, 2021.

———. *Decisions of the Atlanta Campaign: The Twenty-One Critical Decisions That Defined the Operation.* Knoxville: University of Tennessee Press, 2019.

———. *Decisions of the 1862 Kentucky Campaign: The Twenty-Seven Critical Decisions That Defined the Operation.* Knoxville: University of Tennessee Press, 2019.

Peterson, Lawrence K. *Confederate Combat Commander: The Remarkable Life of Brigadier General Alfred Jefferson Vaughan Jr.* Knoxville: University of Tennessee Press, 2013.

Savas, Theodore P., and David A. Woodbury, eds. *The Campaign for Atlanta and Sherman's March to the Sea*. Campbell, CA: Savas Woodbury, 1994.

Scaife, William R. *The Campaign for Atlanta*. 4th ed. Cartersville, GA: Civil War Publications, 1993.

———. *The Chattahoochee River Line: An American Maginot*. Cartersville, GA: Civil War Publications, 2004.

Symonds, Craig L. *Joseph E. Johnston: A Civil War Biography*. New York: W. W. Norton, 1992.

———. *Stonewall of the West: Patrick Cleburne & the Civil War*. Lawrence: University Press of Kansas, 1997.

United States Army. *Dictionary of United States Army Terms*. Washington, DC: United States Government Printing Office, 1983.

Warner, Ezra J. *Generals in Blue: Lives of the Union Commanders*. Baton Rouge: Louisiana State University Press, 1964.

———. *Generals in Gray: Lives of the Confederate Commanders*. Baton Rouge: Louisiana State University Press, 1959.

Weber, Thomas. *The Northern Railroads in the Civil War, 1861–1865*. Bloomington: Indiana University Press, 1952.

Woodworth, Steven E. *Decision in the Heartland: The Civil War in the West*. Westport, CT: Praeger, 2008.

———. *Jefferson Davis and His Generals: The Failure of Confederate Command in the West*. Lawrence: University Press of Kansas, 1990.

———. *Nothing but Victory: The Army of the Tennessee, 1861–1865*. New York: Alfred A. Knopf, 2005.

———. *Sherman*. New York: Palgrave Macmillan, 2009.

INDEX

Page numbers in **boldface** refer to illustrations. Ranks reflect officer's attainment at the time of the Battle of Kennesaw Mountain.

Abatis, 26
Allatoona Mountains, GA, 12
Allatoona Pass, GA, 12; Battle of, 67
Andersonville, GA, 65
Antietam (or Sharpsburg), MD, Battle of, 2
Appomattox Court House, VA, 69
Army of Northern Virginia, CSA, 2, 36, 68–69
Army of Tennessee, CSA, 5, 9–10, 15, 23, 26, 59, 64–65, 68–69
Army of the Cumberland, USA, 21, 65
Army of the Ohio (Twenty-Third Corps), USA, 3, 5, 21, 32–33, 38, 65, 67–68
Army of the Potomac, USA, 1–2, 10
Army of the Tennessee, USA, 9, 12, 21, 60, 65, 67
Army of Virginia, USA, 2

Artillery
—Bellamy's Alabama Battery, CSA, 30
—Guibor's Missouri Battery, CSA, 30
—Hoskin's Mississippi Battery, CSA, 30
—Lumsden's Alabama Battery, CSA, 30
—Mebane's Tennessee Battery, CSA, 27
—Perry's Florida Battery, CSA, 27
—Phelan's Alabama Battery, CSA, 27
—Storrs's Artillery Battalion, CSA, 28
—Ward's Alabama Battery, CSA, 30
Atlanta, Battle of, 64
Atlanta, GA, 30, 62, 64–67
Atlanta and West Point Railroad, 67
Atlanta Campaign, 10, 15–16, 26, 31, 41, 62–63

Baird, Absalom, Brig. Gen., USA, division of, 46
Bald (Leggett's) Hill, GA, 66

Index

Beauregard, P. G. T., Gen., CSA, 5
Belmont, MO, Battle of, 3
Big Black River Bridge, MS, Battle of, 7
Bragg, Braxton, Gen., CSA, 5–10, 23
Brushy Mountain, GA, 13, 16, 18
Buckhead, GA, 65
Buell, Don C., USA, 3, 5
Bull Run (or First Manassas), VA: Battle of, 1, 5; Second Battle of, 2
Burnside, Ambrose, Maj. Gen., USA, 2
Burnt Hickory Road, GA, 47, 50

Calhoun, GA, 12
California, 22, 36,
Canister, 27–28
Cartersville, GA, 47
Cassville, GA, 12
Castel, Albert, 40
casualties, 55, 64
Champion Hill, MS, Battle of, 7
Chancellorsville, VA, 2
Chattahoochee River, 60, 62, 64–65
Chattahoochee River Line, 64–65
Chattanooga, TN, 5, 7–10, 26
Cheatham, Benjamin F., Maj. Gen, CSA: pre-battle, 21–22, **23**, 24, 26–27; during battle, 52; post-battle, 66
Cheatham Hill, **20**, 22, 24, 26, 37, 40 44, 46, 50, 52–53, 55, 62
Cheney House, GA, 33
Chevaux-de-frise, 26
Chickamauga, GA, Battle of, 8–9, 36
Chickamauga Creek, GA, 8
Cleburne, Patrick, Maj. Gen., CSA: division of, 44–45, 50, 52; corps of, 67
Cockrell, Francis M., Brig. Gen., CSA, brigade of, 50

Col. Dan McCook Brigade Association, USA, 52
Cold Harbor, VA, Battle of, 3
Columbia, TN, 68
Columbus, KY, 3
column of brigades, 47–48, 50
Confederacy, 1, 16, 23, 68
Corinth, MS, 3, 5
Cox, Jacob D., Brig. Gen., USA, division of, 47
Cumberland Gap, Ky, TN, VA, 5
Cumberland River, 3

Dallas, GA, 13
Dalton, GA, 10, 15, 43
Davis, Jefferson, President, CSA, 1, 5, 10, 16, 36, 64–65, 69
Davis, Jefferson C., Brig. Gen., USA: 48; division of, 44, 46
Dead Angle, **22**, 26–27, 46, 53–57
Decatur, GA, 65–66
Department of East Tennessee, CSA, 5
Department of the Cumberland, USA, 9
Department of the Ohio, USA, 9
Department of the Tennessee, USA, 9

East Coast, 68
Eastern Theater, 1
Emancipation Proclamation, 7
Etowah River, GA, 12
Ezra Church, Battle of, 64, 67

Fairburn, GA, 67
Fifteenth Corps. *See* Logan, John A., Maj. Gen., USA
Fifty-Fourth Ohio, USA, 50
Fifty-Second Ohio, USA, 55
First and Fifteenth Arkansas, CSA, 52
First Tennessee, CSA, 54

Index

Forrest, Nathan B., Maj. Gen., CSA, 68
Fort Donelson, TN, 3
Fort Henry, TN, 2
Fourteenth Corps. *See* Palmer, John M., Maj. Gen., USA
Fourteenth Kentucky, USA, 38
Fourth Corps. *See* Howard, Oliver, O., Maj. Gen., USA
Franklin, TN, 68
Fredericksburg, VA, 2, Battle of, 2
French, Samuel, Maj. Gen., CSA, 28, 30, 50
Fulton, GA, 60, 62

Garrard, Kenner, Brig. Gen., USA, 66
Geary, John W., Brig. Gen., USA, division of, 38,
Georgia, 33, 64, 68
Georgia Railroad, 65
Gettysburg, PA, Battle of, 2, 7, 36
Gibson, Randall L., Brig. Gen., CSA, 30, brigade of, 30
Gilgal Church, GA, 15–16
Grant, Ulysses S., Lieut. Gen., USA, 2–3, 5, 7, 9–10, 32, 44, 60, 64, 67–69

Halleck, Henry W., Maj. Gen., USA, 2, 5, 10, 60, 67
Hardee, William J., Lieut. Gen., CSA, 13; corps of, 20, 32–37, 42, 66
Harker, Charles G., Brig. Gen., USA, 48, 52; brigade of, 44, **46,** 50, 54
Harpeth River, 68
Harrow, William, Brig. Gen., USA, division of, 46–47
Hell Hole, GA, 13
Hill, Benjamin, Senator, CSA, 62
Hindman, Thomas C., Maj. Gen., CSA, 37; division of, 38

Hood, John B., Lieut. Gen., CSA, 31, **35**–38, 43, 65–68; corps of, 18, 30, 34, 40, 42, 64
Hooker, Joseph, Maj. Gen., USA, 2, 9, 21, 40
Horatius, 53, poem, 90–91
Howard, Oliver, O., Maj. Gen., USA, 47–48, 66–67; Fourth Corps, 44, 46, 67

Illinois Monument, **22,** 55

Jackson, MS, 7
Jackson, Thomas J. "Stonewall," CSA, 2
John Ward Creek, GA, 52
Johnston, Albert S., Gen., CSA, 3
Johnston, Joseph E., Gen., CSA: pre-battle, 1, 10, 12, 15–**16,** 18, 20, 24–26, 31–36, 38, 40; during battle, 41–44, 47; postbattle, 57, 59–60, 62–65, 69
Jonesboro, GA, 67; Battle of, 67

Kennesaw Mountain (Big), GA, 18, 18, **20,** 28–**29,** 30–31, 33–35, 37, 44, 46–47, 50, 60, 62, 64
Kennesaw Mountain, Battle of, 15, 18, 24, 31, 40–41, 47, 63–64
Kennesaw Mountain Line, 15, 18, 20–26, 28, 31–35, 37, 41–44, 50, 56–57, 59, 62–64
Kennesaw Mountain Spur, 20, 46, 50. *See also* Pigeon Hill
Kentucky, 5–6, 36
Kimball, Nathan, Brig. Gen., USA, 48; brigade of, 44, 46, 50, 52
Knoxville, TN, 9
Kolb's Farm, Battle of, 15, 31, 33, 35–36, 40, 43

Index

Latimer House, GA, 16
Lee, Robert E., Gen., CSA, 2–3, 8, 16, 59, 68–69
Lee, Stephen D., Lieut. Gen., CSA, 66–67
Lexington, KY, 5
Lick Skillet Road, GA, 66
Lightburn, Joseph, Brig. Gen., USA, brigade of, 47, 50
Lincoln, Abraham, President, USA, 1–2, 7, 10, 67–69
Lincoln Administration, 6
Little Kennesaw Mountain, GA, 18, **20**, 28–30
Logan, John A., Maj. Gen., USA, 66; Fifteenth Corps of, 46–47, 50, 66–68
Longstreet, James, Lieut. Gen., CSA, 8–9, 36
Lookout Mountain, TN, GA, 9
Loring, William W., Maj. Gen., CSA, 18; corps of (formerly Polk's), 28–29
Lost Mountain, GA, 12, 15
Louisville, KY, 5
Lovejoy's Station, GA, 67

Macon and Western Railroad, 67
Maney, George E., Brig. Gen., CSA, **54**; brigade of, 26, 46, 50, 53–54
March to the Sea, 68
Marietta, GA, 18, 28, 30, 34–35, 37, 60
Marietta-Dallas Road, GA, 16, 20, 22, 32
Martin, William H., Lieut. Col., CSA, 52
Marye's Heights, VA, 2
Maryland, 2
McClellan, George B., Maj. Gen., USA, 1–2

McCook, Daniel, Col., USA, **52**, 53, brigade of, 46, 50, 52–53, 55
McMurry, Richard, 21
McPherson, James B., Maj. Gen., USA, 10, 12, 21, 44, 46–47, 50, 60, 65–67
Meade, George, Maj. Gen., USA, 2–3, 10, 64
Mexican-American War, 22
military crest, 24, **25**, 26, 55
Military Division of the Mississippi, USA, 9–10
mirrors, 57
Missionary Ridge, TN, GA, 9
Mississippi River, 3, 7
Mitchell, John G., Col., USA, brigade of, 46, 50, 53, 55
Morgan, James D., Brig. Gen., USA, brigade of, 46
Mud Creek, GA, 16
Mud Creek Line, GA, 13, 15–16, 18, 43
Mud March, 2
Murfreesboro, TN, 6

Nashville, TN, 3, 5, 67–68
New Hope Church, GA, battle of, 12, 44
Newton, John, Brig. Gen., USA, 47–48, division of, 44

Ohio River, 68
Olly's Creek, GA, 47
125th Illinois, USA, 55
121st Ohio, USA, 55
130th Ohio, USA, 55
Oostanaula River, 12, 62
Osterhaus, Peter J., Brig. Gen. USA, division of, 46

Paducah, KY, 3
Palmer, John M., Maj. Gen., USA, 48; Fourteenth Corps, 21, 44, 67–68

Index

Peachtree Creek, 65, Battle of, 64–66
Pemberton, John C., Lieut. Gen., CSA, 7
Pennsylvania, 2
Perryville, KY, Battle of, 5–6
Petersburg, VA, 3
Pickett-Pettigrew-Trimble Charge, 68
Pickett's Mill, GA, Battle of, 13, 44
Pigeon Hill, 20, 28, 46, 50
Pine Mountain, GA, 13, 16
Pittsburg Landing, TN, 3
Polk, Leonidas, Lieut. Gen., CSA, 3 5–6, 13
Polk, Lucius, Brig. Gen., CSA, brigade of, 44
Polk's (Loring's) Corps, CSA, 18
Pope, John, Maj. Gen., USA, 2
Powder Springs Road, GA, 20, 33, 35–38, 44
Preliminary Emancipation Proclamation, 2
Presstman, Stephen W., Lieut. Col., CSA, 20–21

Rappahannock River, VA, 1–2
Reconstruction, 69
Reed's Bridge, GA, 8
Resaca, GA, 12, 43, 62; Battle of, 12, 44
Richmond, KY, Battle of, 5
Richmond, VA, 1–2, 36, 69
Rocky Face Ridge, GA, 10
Rosecrans, William S., Maj. Gen., USA, 6–9
Roswell, GA, 65
Ruff's Mill, GA, 64

Sandtown Road, GA, 13
Savannah, GA, 68

Schofield, John M., Maj. Gen., USA, 21, 33, 44, 47, 62
Seven Pines (or Fair Oaks), VA, Battle of, 2
Seventeenth Corps, USA, 47, 50, 67
Sherman, Ellen, 63
Sherman, William T., Maj. Gen., USA: pre-battle, 9–10, 12, 15, 18, **21**, 24, 31–35, 40; during battle, 41–44, 47, 50, 55; postbattle, 57, 59–60, 62–64, 66–69
Shiloh (or Pittsburg Landing), TN, Battle of, 5
Shoup, Francis A., Brig. Gen., CSA, 28, 65–66
Shoupades, 64
Sixteenth Corps, USA, 47, 50, 68
Smith, Edmund Kirby, Maj. Gen., CSA, 5–6
Smith, Giles A., Brig. Gen., USA, brigade of, 47, 50
Smith, John E., Brig. Gen., USA, division of, 46–47
Smith, Morgan L., Brig. Gen., USA, division of, 46–47
Smyrna, GA, 60
Smyrna Campground, GA, 64
Smyrna Line, 62
Snake Creek Gap, GA, 10
South Carolina, 68
Special Field Orders Number 28, 44
Spotsylvania Court House, VA, Battle of, 3, 64
Spring Hill, TN, 68
Stevenson, Carter L., Maj. Gen., CSA, 37; division of, 38, 40
Stewart, Alexander P., Maj. Gen., CSA, 37; division of, 38, 40
Stones River, TN, Battle of, 6–7, 23

Storrs, George S., Maj., CSA, 28, 30
Tennessee, 5–6, 68
Tennessee River, 3, 7, 68
Texas, 36
Thomas, George, Maj. Gen., USA, 8–10, 21, 44, 47, 55, 65, 67–68
topographical crest, 24–**25,** 26, 55
Tullahoma Campaign, 7
Tunnel, **56**
Tupelo, MS, 5, 68
Twentieth (Hooker's) Corps, USA, 21, 32–33, 38, 67–68
Twenty-Third New York, USA, 38

US War Department, 69

Vaughan, Alfred J Jr., Brig. Gen., CSA, 26, **53**–54; brigade of, 27, 46, 50, 53
Vicksburg, MS, 7
Virginia, 2, 59–60, 68

Wagner, George D., Brig. Gen., USA, brigade of, 44, 46, 50, 52
Walcutt, Charles C., Brig. Gen., USA, brigade of, 47, 50
Wangelin, Hugo, Col., USA, brigade of, 46
Washington, DC, 1–2, 10
Watkins, Samuel, Pvt., CSA, 54
West Point (US Military Academy), NY, 3, 16, 36, 59
Western and Atlantic Railroad, 10, 12, 18, 30, 37, 42, 67
Western Theater, 3
Wheeler's Cavalry, CSA, 35, 42, 66
Wilderness, VA, Battle of, 3, 64
Williams, Alpheus, S., Brig. Gen., USA, division of, 38
Williamson, James A., Col., USA, brigade of, 46
Woods, Charles R., Brig. Gen., USA, brigade of, 46
Work, J. B., 52